THE FLOATING WORLD
IN JAPANESE FICTION

THE FLOATING WORLD
IN JAPANESE FICTION

THE FLOATING WORLD
IN
JAPANESE FICTION

HOWARD HIBBETT

CHARLES E. TUTTLE COMPANY
Rutland, Vermont & Tokyo, Japan

Published by the Charles E. Tuttle Company, Inc.
of Rutland, Vermont & Tokyo, Japan
with editorial offices at
Suido 1-chome, 2-6, Bunkyo-ku, Tokyo, Japan
by special arrangement with
Oxford University Press, London

Copyright in Japan, 1959, by Oxford University Press

International Standard Book No. 0-8048-1154-7

First edition, 1959 by
Oxford University Press, London
First Tuttle edition, 1975
Sixth printing, 1989

PRINTED IN JAPAN

TO
Serge Elisséeff

PREFACE

JAPANESE literature is so often identified with certain of its traditional forms—courtly romances, the mysterious *nō* plays, delicate miniature poems about a falling leaf or a fading flower —that it has been sometimes unjustly disparaged for its limitations. Cherry blossoms are not the preoccupation of all its writers; nor is their mood invariably one of wistful melancholy. In particular, quite different views will be found to colour seventeenth- and eighteenth-century fiction, the literary counterpart of the familiar *ukiyo-e*, or 'pictures of the floating world'.

The fiction of the floating world belonged to a prosperous, creative, and illegitimate élite. It was an élite of shopkeepers and entertainers, at the bottom of the Japanese feudal order. But fashionable opinion had prejudices of its own, not the official ones, and the *ukiyo*—the 'floating world' of Kyoto, Osaka, and Edo—had become fashionable by the Genroku Era (roughly, 1680 to 1730 or 1740, though the name comes from the year-period 1688–1703). With money, a fishmonger's son could be a social lion. Careers of beauty were never more accessible. An obscure shop or tea-house might blossom into splendid profit; whereupon its owner would 'train an epicure's palate, renew his wardrobe, and yearn for the exquisite in all things'. And his parties would begin to include celebrated actors and courtesans, with expensive tastes.

Here, then, are a few members of this Genroku café society as they appear in the *ukiyo-zōshi*, or 'tales of the floating world'. The West has been accustomed to look at their world only in the *ukiyo-e* woodcuts—not in the *ukiyo-zōshi*, its popular fiction. Yet, as we see in the history of the illustrated book, these arts were intimately allied. Both offer pictures of the floating world— images drawn from the same milieu of shop, street, theatre, and tea-house, and reflecting the same poses, the same cosmetic chic, the same glossy coiffures and showy dresses in striped, checked, or flowered fabrics. Of course there is a difference in point of view. Authors were in the habit of lecturing the worldly, or being witty at their expense; while print designers were more often content to admire beauty where they found it. The *ukiyo-e* designer wishes above all to make a handsome composition of line and mass; the *ukiyo-zōshi* writer, with his black umbrella of didactic theory, prefers to satirize, to parody, and to caricature. And so their sketches, graphic and literary, illuminate each other, and the figures of the *ukiyo* stand out more sharply in this cross-lighting.

To be sure, these are not live, fully rounded characters, nor even impeccable wax figures from a Japanese Madame Tussaud's. Since the Genroku writer does not attempt to create the illusion of reality, whatever life his fiction may seem to have is indeed its own. Like the prints, Genroku stories and novels have a somewhat eccentric charm. In the first half of this book, therefore, I have tried to explain some of the conventions of *ukiyo* fiction, and its relation to the art of *ukiyo-e*, as well as to introduce Saikaku and Kiseki, the leading authors, and the society in which they lived. A study of these aspects of Genroku culture, besides its literary and historical interest, should help to enhance appreciation of the *ukiyo-e.* In this way, too, I hope to provide a suitable background for the translations that follow. Without such tales as these, Japanese social and cultural history would lack one of its richest sources. But they are not simply documents. *Ukiyo-zōshi* were written for the casual reader, who, after two centuries, may still find them entertaining. As with the prints, their appreciation requires chiefly a willingness to forgo the illusionistic conventions of Western realism, rather than detailed knowledge of their exotic background.

Certainly a great deal more could be said to introduce Kiseki's naughty young men and women, or to annotate Saikaku's amazing epitome of harlotry, *The Woman Who Spent Her Life in Love*. Nearly every line of these tales would serve as the text for a sermon-length footnote. But much can be read in the illustrations and between the lines. A formal introduction, punctilious in its detail, seems as out of place as a chaperon at a Yoshiwara party.

CONTENTS

Part One
The *Ukiyo-zōshi* and the Floating World

Part Two
Figures of the Floating World

CONTENTS

ILLUSTRATIONS

xi

ACKNOWLEDGEMENTS

I AM indebted to the following institutions for permission to use photographs made from books in their collections: Art Institute of Chicago (Plate I); Museum of Fine Arts, Boston (II–V); Tokyo University Library and Tenri University Library (VI); Oriental Library of the University of California, Berkeley (VIII, X–XIV); Waseda University Library (IX); Tōyō Bunko, Tokyo (XV–XXIV). The Charles E. Tuttle Co. has kindly granted permission to quote from W. T. de Bary, tr., *Five Women Who Loved Love*.

I should like to thank Dr. Richard Lane and Dr. Burton Watson for their criticism of the manuscript; I am grateful, too, for the generous help given me by Professor Noma Kōshin of Kyoto University, Professor Konishi Jin'ichi of Tokyo Educational University, and, in particular, the teacher under whose guidance I began this study and to whom I dedicate it.

PART ONE

The *Ukiyo-zōshi* and the Floating World

I

GENROKU

JAPANESE fiction of the Genroku Era (that is, of the late seventeenth and early eighteenth centuries) has an impressive ancestry which can be traced back to the Heian Court. Unfortunately, its own reputation is scandalous. For years its authors were not received in the polite company of Literature, nor were their books conspicuous in proper households. Saikaku, Kiseki, and the others had written for amusement, if not simply for money. Their tone was often cheerfully indecent, their moralizing superficial at best. And they had debased the art of fiction by portraying the *ukiyo*, the 'floating world' of transient pleasures, a world in which society was led by the wrong set. 'The deplorable fact cannot be concealed—its principal figures were the courtesan and the actor, while among its supernumeraries were the disreputable crowd of pandars and procurers who haunted the gay quarters.' [1] In these circles the Genroku writer found new and exciting characters for fiction. Literature was invaded by all the dashing figures of the floating world: by courtesans, actors, jesters, rakes and dandies, offensively rich shopkeepers, their spoiled sons and daughters, and their vain, luxurious wives.

Persons of this interesting but dubious sort thus became the favourite subject of the *ukiyo-zōshi*, those often pornographic 'tales of the floating world'. They figured also in the contemporary *ukiyo-e* woodcut, an unrespectable offshoot of painting, as well as in songs, ballads, and the colourfully staged plays of a new popular theatre, the *kabuki*. Of course the prosperous Genroku pleasure-seekers, with their entertainers and their hangers-on, made up only a small part of the urban population; and throughout the long rule of the Tokugawa Shogunate (1600–1868) their official position in society was extremely low. But already in Genroku the members of this curious élite enjoyed considerable freedom, within the rigid framework of a

3

highly organized feudal society. They were freed both by the contempt of strict social dogma, which tried to ignore their obvious importance, and by the operation of still stricter economic laws. Pauper or merchant prince, all except samurai and peasants (and the comparative few who belonged to the clergy, to the old court nobility, or to outcast groups) were lumped together as *chōnin*: 'townsmen'.

Chōnin, then, was the indiscriminate, often insulting term for people of the artisan and trading classes, who alone profited from the trend to luxury. Among them were shopkeepers and craftsmen of all kinds, their clerks and their apprentices, as well as a few rich merchants, brokers, wholesalers, and powerful moneylenders whose clientele included feudal lords (*daimyō*) throughout Japan. In the floating world each enjoyed prestige according to his means—and taste. Yet the samurai, the aloof warrior of the ruling military class, thought of townsmen, if at all, as vulgar, parasitic rascals, corrupted by handling money. According to a convenient Chinese theory they ranked below even the most wretched peasant, since he had the essential task of producing rice. But peasants were warned to eat coarse grain instead of their own rice, to divorce a wife who was overly fond of tea, to abstain from *sake*, and to get up early, cut grass in the morning, till the fields all day, and spend the evening making straw ropes and sacks. For the townsman there were rather different rules. As early as 1649 he was told not to wear silk, live in a three-storeyed house, decorate his rooms with gold and silver leaf, or furnish them with objects of gold lacquer. Such rules, elaborated and insistently repeated, at last compose a negative image of Genroku extravagance.[2]

Townsmen had to be reminded of their inferiority; for the growth of mercantilism, and of a complex financial system that the Tokugawa Government found quite baffling, had in fact made them a privileged class. The profits of a wildly fluctuating market streamed into their storehouses, while the Government was busy trying to dam the flow—and protect its artificial social order—by a wall of edicts. But Tokugawa officials failed to work out an adequate tax system. Instead, they spent their time drawing up vague, lofty Confucian exhortations, or devising laws of extreme pettiness, as if to forbid everything that was not compulsory. Both were difficult to enforce. During the seventeenth century townsmen prospered—and were grateful, after the long medieval wars, for the peace and stability of Tokugawa rule.

Chōnin strength was still concentrated in Kyoto and Osaka, the two great cities of western Japan. But Edo, the Shogun's new capital, had begun to fill out some of the wards of the modern Tokyo, foreshadowing its domination of the entire country. Already Edo was the centre of government and of military power, one of the three largest cities, the boom town of the newest *nouveaux riches*. In the arts Edo offered a robust style of *kabuki* theatre, suited to its own brash, upstart temperament, and a thriving school of *ukiyo-e* print-makers. Here, Moronobu designed his vivacious woodcuts—pictures of the floating world of Edo streets and shops, and particularly of that prime Edo tourist attraction, the Yoshiwara.

Yet *ukiyo-e* and *kabuki*, to say nothing of *ukiyo* literature, had begun in Kyoto, the ancient capital. For nearly a thousand years this Chinese-plan metropolis had been the seat of the Emperor's Court, which assured its authority in arts and manners. It also shared in the new wealth, as Saikaku observes in a story published in 1686:

When you look out over the present Kyoto from the west gate of Kiyomizu Temple, you see such long, crowded rows of white-walled storehouses that in summer, in the early sunlight, the city sparkles as if on a snowy morning. The opulence of the era is manifested by silent pines,[3] and by cranes diverting themselves among the clouds. In the time of Nobunaga [4] there were said to be 98,000 houses in this endlessly swelling city; now, even those embankments where bamboo groves stood have been swallowed up by the capital. Smoke rises, morning and night, from the kitchen fires of all sorts of tradesmen.

Even the learned and cosmopolitan Engelbert Kaempfer, who visited Kyoto a few years later during his service with the Dutch East India Company, was impressed by this aspect of 'Miaco' (Miyako, the capital). In his *History of Japan* Kaempfer wrote:

Miaco is the great magazine of all Japanese manufactures and commodities, and the chief mercantile town in the Empire. There is scarce a house in this large capital where there is not something made or sold. Here they refine copper, coin money, print books,

5

weave the richest stuffs with gold and silver flowers. The best and scarcest dies, the most artful carvings, all sorts of musical Instruments, pictures, japan'd cabinets, all sorts of things wrought in gold and other metals, particularly in steel, as the best temper'd blades, and other arms are made here in the utmost perfection, as are also the richest dresses, and after the best fashion, all sorts of toys, puppets, moving their heads of themselves, and numberless other things, too many to be here mention'd. In short, there is nothing that can be thought of, but what may be found at Miaco . . . [5]

And Kaempfer saw that Osaka, the centre of the rice trade and the young business rival of Kyoto, was also 'well inhabited by rich merchants, artificers and manufacturers'. Though not so large as Edo and Kyoto, which were cities of more than half a million, Osaka dominated Japanese commerce at this time. Furthermore, it deserved its reputation for gaiety, and for free spending:

Even what tends to promote luxury, and to gratify all sensual pleasures, may be had at as easy a rate here as any where. For this reason the Japanese call Osacca the universal theatre of pleasures and diversions. . . . Hence it is no wonder, that numbers of strangers and travellers daily resort thither, chiefly rich people, as to a place, where they can spend their time and money with much greater satisfaction, than perhaps any where else in the Empire. [6]

In all of the 'three cities' townsmen were prospering. They, too, had begun to spend a great deal of money on luxuries—clothing of gorgeous fabrics, lacquer ware, screens, tea-bowls, books, and prints. Business methods helped in supplying all their wants: artists and craftsmen began to work for customers instead of patrons. Urged on by a fresh spirit of rivalry in display (and doubtless by more effective methods of sales promotion), the townsmen poured out much of their sudden wealth in a carnival extravagance. Tales of conspicuous consumption are common in the literature of the time, along with accounts of spectacular wealth among the powerful merchants. The house of Yodoya, which was at last punished for its arrogance, is reported to have had among its many treasures: thousands of rolls of silks, brocades, and velvets; hundreds of swords, screens, carpets, paintings, and precious tea-bowls; ninety-six sliding doors of crystal; jewels of all kinds; and—to mention only one

of its objects in solid gold—a chessboard three inches thick.[7]
The modes of city life had proliferated, and successful merchants filled their storehouses with things too costly for many of
their superiors. To these townsmen, at least, Genroku was an
age in which cranes might well circle auspiciously over silent
pines. The rich could afford to indulge their taste for luxuries
of whatever kind.

Moreover, their pursuit of happiness, which they were inclined to identify with luxurious pleasures, was not greatly
inhibited either by legislation or by the influence of the samurai
code—itself far more lenient, in some respects, than the stern
Calvinist ethic so important to Western economic growth.
Spending money, whether on art and literature or *sake* and
women, might be unwise for its practical consequences, but
it was not considered sinful. In such an atmosphere new and
comparatively unrestrained cultural forms could thrive;
and, along with the springtime excesses of the *ukiyo*, there was
a real flowering of its lively arts. This 'modest renaissance',
as Sir George Sansom has called it,[8] was at its height from
about 1680 to 1740, the some half-dozen decades known as
'Genroku'.

Specifically, the era-name Genroku, chosen as auspicious for
a new reign, was adopted in the ninth moon of the year corresponding to 1688. It was the year after the accession of the
Emperor Higashiyama, the 113th Sovereign of Japan, a child of
thirteen whose quiet, ceremonial-burdened Kyoto life was conducted in what Kaempfer describes as 'a splendid poverty'.[9]
More important, it was the eighth year of the rule of Tsunayoshi, fifth Tokugawa Shogun; and his political position was as
strong as his vast Edo castle, with its concentric moats and
walls. If the ills of the Shogunate were already chronic, they
were not yet acute. As usual, there were financial troubles:
besides indulging in a sybaritic private life, ornamented by
handsome pages and *nō* dancers, Tsunayoshi was very generous,
especially in pious causes, and 'built and repaired Shinto
shrines and Buddhist temples apparently at random'.[10] But
money could easily be had by imposing special taxes, selling
monopolies, or (what soon became a favourite panacea) de-
basing the currency. The institutions established by the first
three Shoguns were functioning admirably. No threat to them,

internal or external, could be discerned. Feudal control had been centralized under the military government, or 'Bakufu', of the Tokugawa house; and this new, more efficient system of oppression was taken for granted as the normal order of society. Although the wars of the medieval period were only a romantic memory, the military class still held its ideals of duty and *noblesse oblige*—its swords no longer quite so sharp, perhaps, but always at hand, ready to defend the status quo against whatever enemies might appear.

There seemed to be no danger from abroad, however, either from China or the West; and within Japan none of the other lords could challenge the Shogun. Obviously the townspeople and peasants held no revolutionary threat. They were disarmed, formed into self-policing 'joint responsibility' groups, indoctrinated with the proper notions of their place in society— and subject, moreover, to surveillance by Bakufu secret agents, as well as by the idle, prolific samurai. There had been no uprising for half a century: none since the Shogunate had adopted its near-hermetic policy of Seclusion, which allowed only a few Dutch and Chinese traders—unlikely to proselytize or do anything that might spoil their trade—in the remote southern port of Nagasaki. After considerable experience at foreign trade, piracy, and military aggression on a precociously modern scale, Japan had withdrawn into complete insularity.

Possibly it was felt that the people of the continent, and the intrusive Westerners, were the ones who had been isolated. Though narrowly confined, the Japanese had rich cultural resources for an introspective life. The Seclusion policy shut out opportunities for further wealth, it was true, but it also kept out dangerous ideas, which might have led to change. No doubt the Tokugawa system would last for ever, sustained by its matchless power and by a vigorous, self-sufficient economy. To those who wished foreign novelties the Nagasaki traders could supply as many as the Bakufu allowed; others would find all they needed or desired, however costly, among the excellent products of Japanese arts and crafts. These were already abundant at Edo, which had become a city only after Ieyasu, the first Tokugawa Shogun, had established his headquarters there less than a century before. But Edo, in the first year of Genroku, was not yet the artistic and commercial centre of Japan.

Kyoto, where Kiseki was then a fashionable young man, and particularly Osaka, where Saikaku had published a dozen *ukiyo-zōshi* by that year, were still very prosperous. Their shops supplied goods of every kind, from fans to armour, for anyone who could afford them, and their entertainers helped to keep the profits in circulation.

In 1704 the era-name was changed from Genroku to Hōei, after Edo suffered a ravaging earthquake and fire. By that time the crest of Tokugawa prosperity may have passed. Yet trade went on briskly, the gaiety of the *ukiyo* continued, and nothing seemed to menace the political and social stability to which the Shogunate was dedicated. The most stirring event of Genroku, and indeed of the Tokugawa Period, was the famous vendetta and suicide of the 'forty-seven *rōnin*', which soon became a hackneyed, irresistible subject for stories, plays, and prints. But any minor feud between samurai clans could infect the whole country with its excitement. Under the martial law of Tokugawa a private revenge had the drama of a revolution.

Even when the term Genroku is extended to include most of the first half of the eighteenth century (as it commonly is), these wider boundaries enclose little more historical incident than the usual fires, floods, earthquakes, differences in administration, and more or less subtle social and economic changes. The eighth Shogun, Yoshimune, who ruled from 1716 to 1745, began a strong reform movement which had the effect of restoring the value of the coinage for a time, improving the archery and swordsmanship of his retainers, and encouraging such virtues as studiousness and frugality. Later Shoguns followed their own inclinations, often paid for by debasement of the coinage. Economic forces were not checked by the monotonous, high-minded edicts, and pressures against the Bakufu steadily increased. Doubtless the political aspects of Tokugawa history are undramatic, if not dull, compared with the wars and revolutions of Europe during those two and a half centuries. Its culture invites attention, however, and not merely for the phenomenon of a protracted medievalism. If we cannot find parallels to the great contemporary European movements, from Baroque to Romanticism, there is nevertheless an interesting, though arrested, development towards what we may call a modern culture. This tendency reached an early climax in the

Genroku Era, when the expansive spirit of the townsmen began rushing out through every chink, crack, and narrow window of its feudal prison.

Of course this 'Genroku spirit' was identified only after it had been dissipated. Its essence was an unreflective enjoyment of the moment—a moment valued for present pleasure, but to be savoured with discrimination. It may even remind us of the more tenuous refinement of the Heian courtier, as portrayed some seven centuries before in *The Tale of Genji*. The *ukiyo* élite, of wealth or talent though not of birth, cherished a similar regard for whatever was newest in the arts, as well as for the casual virtuoso who could improvise beautifully. But Genroku artists were thorough-going professionals. Saikaku and Kiseki turned out best-sellers regularly; Chikamatsu produced plays to order, sometimes within a few weeks; actors, dancers, and musicians were trained from childhood, and belonged to hereditary schools with carefully preserved traditions. Even the lonely, meditative poet Bashō trained a school of followers, and earned his livelihood by teaching his poetic art. The purpose of long training was to combine spontaneity and skill, through a mastery of traditional techniques. The painter had a repertoire of effects, and worked very swiftly; poets, as well as story-tellers, were ready to improvise on any suitable theme. Indeed, the chief poetic form of the age was a kind of linked-verse, composed extemporaneously by a group of poets following certain precise rules.

Genroku social life had these characteristics too: the code of manners observed in the pleasure quarter, where one escaped the Confucian proprieties, was a thorny set of unwritten rules, designed for the connoisseur. In the cultures of both Genroku and Heian, though one may be called *bourgeois* and the other courtly, there is a deep respect for etiquette. Yet both have an engagingly youthful verve, for all their elaboration; one might, less kindly, describe them as immature. In particular, the people of the *ukiyo* seldom display an appreciation of abstract thought, or an adult sense of gravity. Their artists—those of the *ukiyo-zōshi* and the *ukiyo-e*, at least—show the bright figures, costumes, and settings of the floating world in an atmosphere unclouded by moral and intellectual preoccupations.

In Genroku the *ukiyo* itself—the world of pleasure, of the

pursuit of money necessary to enjoy it, and of the instability that underlay all—was still an exciting discovery. Only since the beginning of the seventeenth century had the word *ukiyo* become more than a reminder of the brevity and uncertainty of life. By mid-century it had acquired such meanings as 'modern', 'up to date', 'fashionable', or even 'fast'. It was prefixed to the names of all sorts of novelties, from dolls to dumplings. '*Ukiyo*-madness' was an addiction to visiting the pleasure quarter; piquant gossip was called '*ukiyo*-talk'; popular songs, of the kind sung by courtesans, were known as '*ukiyo*-tunes'. Above all, *ukiyo* meant the life of pleasure, accepted without thinking what might lie ahead. In Asai Ryōi's *Tales of the Floating World* [11] (*c.* 1661) it is defined as living for the moment, gazing at the moon, snow, blossoms, and autumn leaves, enjoying wine, women, and song, and, in general, drifting with the current of life 'like a gourd floating downstream'.[12] Still, *ukiyo* retained the overtones of its earlier Buddhist use to suggest the sad impermanence of earthly things. The Chinese had also used it to imply the transiency of life, as in a line by the T'ang poet Li Shang-yin: 'In this floating world there are many meetings and partings.' And even Saikaku, who was not often melancholy, gave it that sense in the first of his erotic novels (themselves called '*ukiyo*-books'): 'Alive today in this floating world, tomorrow I may end as sea-wrack on the rough shore of Oya-shirazu.' [13] The same poignant word begins his death verse, which observes that he has lived two years beyond the normal span of fifty:

Ukiyo no tsuki	The moon of this floating world
misugoshinikeri	Has lingered in view . . .
sue ninen	Two years.

But *ukiyo* usually suggests the buoyant exhilaration of the Genroku spirit, rather than its underlying awareness that life is fleeting. Zest for the current fashions made it hard to think that another season, possibly not so brilliant, would overthrow them.

The people of the *ukiyo* disliked whatever they thought to be outmoded. When a tradition had vitality, they followed it. But antiquarianism and historical interests were left to those (priests, samurai, and members of the Court nobility) who had the mixed pleasure of recalling their glorious past. Of course the ordinary citizens of Genroku were not entitled to share this heritage, and for later townsmen there was only the comparatively recent memory of the Genroku Era itself, the few seventeenth- and early eighteenth-century decades in which their city culture had flowered. Yet as Heian was the golden age of the Court, Kamakura the most splendid in military tradition, and Muromachi the time when the Buddhist clergy was at its highest eminence—so Genroku had a special lustre for succeeding generations of actors, courtesans, and tradesmen. It was then, they felt, that the new prosperity of the cities had reached its zenith: then, fortunes were made overnight, luxury was profuse, and the arts (if not so sophisticated) were at their most vigorous.

To modern Japanese, Genroku seems to have been a gilded age of prosperity, light-heartedness, and pleasure. It is true that this agreeable view of Genroku, myopically focused on its wealth and gaiety and often tawdry glamour, omits the grey realities of ordinary city life under an extraordinarily oppressive social and political system. But the view itself is real enough—perhaps more vivid than English memories of Edwardian ease—and it colours the whole vague nostalgic feeling for the Tokugawa Period. Intellectuals find it hard to give up this illusion; fervent members of the *avant-garde* reveal a weakness for the *kabuki* theatre, where something of the Edo past can be recaptured. And the idea of a golden past is not entirely illusory. As even the disenchanted will agree, Genroku was the meridian of an age when a great many unpleasant problems had not yet been discovered.

Indeed, Genroku was at once a time of oppression and one when the tinsel of city life—the picnics, boating parties, rich fabrics and gaudy theatrical posters, lantern festivals and fireworks—glittered with special brilliance. It *was* an opulent age. Well-to-do merchants lived as ostentatiously as they dared, and, for the rest, spent their money on unobtrusive luxuries—choice foods, plain kimono with princely linings, exquisitely carved *netsuke* to fasten a coin purse, or a gold-lacquer pill-box, to the sash. If sculpture had to be small, they felt, it could have microscopic finesse: hence the marvellous tiny world of ivory, horn, or boxwood animals and human figures. Miniature art, whether in hair ornaments or sword fittings, dolls or dwarf trees, became the object of intense connoisseurship.

Architecture, at the other extreme, made no great progress except in refinement and sophistication of detail. There was little support for it from the newly rich: an imposing house might annoy the Bakufu, or be destroyed in one of the fires that so often swept through these wooden cities. Of the few townsmen who could afford a mansion, and a spacious garden with stones, streams, pools, rare trees, and a tea pavilion, fewer still cared to make this sort of display. It was safer to invest in works of art, handsome clothing, and expensive furnishings; these were kept in the fireproof *kura* (a storehouse with white-plastered mud walls and a tiled roof), from which they were brought out for occasional use. Among the contents of a storehouse, besides whatever money and merchandise was on hand, there were always scrolls of painting and calligraphy, and ceramics suitable for decorating the *tokonoma* alcove or using in the tea ceremony; there might also be such treasures as a lacquer ink-stone box by Kōetsu or Kōrin, a magnificent pair of folding screens (a classic landscape, a scene from *Genji*, gnarled plum branches in black ink on a refulgent ground), or perhaps a single tea-bowl of subdued colour, irregular shape, and delicious texture, more valuable than the sum of all the other possessions.

There, too, would be kept the indispensable luxury: fine garments. And Genroku fashion required a very large wardrobe. At a picnic to look at flowers, for instance, a lady would not only dress as elegantly as possible, and see that her attendants did so, in their way; but she would also have servants bring along a carpet, a wind curtain to be hung between the trees, a set of lacquer boxes for food, cosmetics, and other supplies, and a few extra gowns so that she need not spend a whole afternoon in the same costume. The spare kimono, which were no less luxurious, would be draped casually over the curtain, or in place of it, presumably to help screen her from public view as she sat admiring some especially pretty blossoms. To judge from the variety and vividness of the patterns, as seen in contemporary fashion books and *ukiyo-e* prints, it must have been painfully evident when a woman wore (or displayed) the same gown too often. For she chose brightly coloured satin, damask,

I. Sukenobu: *Picture Book of the Pine Tree*

Under the cherry blossoms. An attendant (herself in a kimono decorated with plovers, waves, and reed fish-weirs) hangs one elaborate kimono over the wind curtain; while her mistress, who has just changed from it, ties her

cloud-patterned sash over another (*nanten* leaves and flowers on a light field alternating with dotted clouds in black). The wind curtain bears a design of paulownia leaves, flying plovers, and a winding stream. A rush hat (worn on flower-viewing excursions and other outings) hangs from a branch above the picture.

and crêpe silks, and had them elaborately dyed, woven, embroidered (often in metallic threads), or hand-painted, preferably by an artist of the first rank. Their patterns included abstract designs, sometimes of startling boldness, clouds, castles, mountains, rivers, trees and flowers of all kinds, and of course such familiar combinations as cranes and pines, lions and peonies, *shō-chiku-bai* (pine, bamboo and plum), and the 'seven plants' of autumn.[14]

Genroku men of fashion dressed as fastidiously as the women, if in more sober colours; and even shop clerks could enjoy the resplendent costumes and décor of the *kabuki* stage. Prodigious sums went for finery and entertainment. Perhaps the increasing sale of books, prints, clothing, perfumes, and theatre tickets has less economic significance than the state of the rice market. But it reveals something of the culture. Records show that there were 1,304 rice-brokers in Osaka as early as 1626: fortunately they also mention that there were fifty bookshops, fifteen theatres, and (it must be admitted) thirty-one brothels.[15]

To be sure, *ukiyo* art and literature were not the pure products of a shopkeepers' culture. Certain aristocratic traditions had filtered down to them; others were introduced directly by writers and artists of samurai origin who had crossed the neat lines drawn by the Bakufu. Society was by no means fluid; yet a wealthy merchant could find a son-in-law of high rank; and an average samurai, still more easily, could drift into the lower classes, or into disreputable artistic circles. Bashō, Chikamatsu, and a number of lesser writers came from military families, as did Koryūsai and Eishi among other *ukiyo-e* designers. Indeed, one of the most important groups in shaping Genroku culture was that of the *rōnin*, or 'wave-men'—masterless samurai who had joined the floating population of the cities. Many *rōnin* earned their living as teachers, not only of riding, archery, and the like, but also of philosophy, calligraphy, Chinese literature, and other learned subjects, such as both Ieyasu and Tsunayoshi had urged them to pursue. Often their pupils were ambitious townsmen, eager to equip themselves and their families for social climbing. When a samurai needed money, as he now frequently did, he was disposed to forget the indignity of patronage by townsmen.

Thus the cultural history of Genroku illustrates at once the rise of a new society and its reinforcement from conservative ranks. The fact that sound businessmen were anxious about their handwriting, if not their versification in Chinese, may help to explain why the growth of this urban culture was not accompanied by a corresponding decay in the old traditions. Japanese artistic, literary, and social forms have always been tenacious. In Genroku, the traditional courtly styles of painting, poetry, calligraphy, and music were still expertly practised; and the arts patronized by the Muromachi Shoguns—the *nō* drama, and the tea ceremony, with its ancillary arts of ceramics and flower-arrangement—were still cultivated by Tokugawa samurai and their lords. These elegancies, so far from the usual 'popular' taste, also appealed to many townsmen, though not entirely for aesthetic reasons. A very rich merchant might have a *nō* stage in his house, after the fashion of a *daimyō*; and his wife, when dressed to visit a temple or to go 'flower-viewing', would be likely to out-dazzle a *daimyō*'s lady. According to Kiseki, a merchant's son might cultivate aristocratic tastes of all sorts ('As he gazed at flowers, he selected rhymes for Chinese poems'); and no affectation was too far-fetched to be often seen. Even the *recherché* pastime of incense-guessing came into vogue.

No doubt these were acquired tastes, as Kiseki's sketches imply; but they were often extremely rarefied ones, and it is surprising how many went to the trouble of acquiring them. The ordinary *ukiyo-zōshi* reader must have been expected to know an allusion when he saw one. Commentaries on the stories of Saikaku, who has been called 'uneducated' by more scholarly (and more pedestrian) authors, yield profuse footnotes to *nō* plays, Japanese and Chinese poetry, and such Heian classics as *The Tales of Ise*, *The Tale of Genji*, and *The Pillow Book*. But *ukiyo-zōshi* writers, who accepted the past without thinking of it as history, tended to use allusion and quotation decoratively (if not humorously or satirically), rather than to give their work another dimension. Their appreciation of beauty, though quick, was not at all reverent; nor did their feeling for Buddhism, which had declined as an institution but was still a strong popular faith, keep them from writing about it in a frivolous or ribald tone, or from making a temple visit an occasion for gaiety. Some of the piquancy of the *ukiyo-zōshi* comes from its curious plebeian–aristocratic mixture of ingredients.

Unlike the solemn *nō* plays or the suave forms of the tea ceremony, then, *ukiyo-zōshi* have the same mixed background as this parvenu but sophisticated Genroku society. And they share its raffish charm, its zest, its resilience even under the heavy Tokugawa pressures. While extolling every Confucian virtue, they display hedonistic, materialistic attitudes. Concrete words are preferred to abstract ideas. Their pages are dense with imagery: images of the ordinary things of life (tubs, rakes, and pruning-shears), and particularly images of luxury (palanquins, splendid clothing, rare tea objects, gold and silver in coins, bars, and sculptured figures). However meagre these lists may be in comparison with actual Genroku inventories, they convey a similar impression of innocent prodigality.

And *ukiyo-zōshi* characters are full of the gusto of an energetic, irrepressibly rising class. The women, for example, are not the frail, languid creatures of a later *ukiyo* style. Robust Genroku beauties do not cultivate the nuance: they paint and powder energetically; their movements have sensuous weight; as courtesans, they betray their amorousness too frankly. In the tales of Saikaku and Kiseki they reveal a brisk, impulsive temperament. Some could hardly be more brazen: arson, adultery, and elopement are among their indiscretions. No doubt such stories have a libellous ring, but there is a great deal of literary evidence to show that meekness was not yet universal among Tokugawa wives and daughters, and that the dashing Genroku spirit was more pervasive than has sometimes been thought. At least it pervades the literature. In Kiseki's longest tirade against modern hussies (at the beginning of *Characters of Worldly Young Women*) he merely assembles and illustrates themes which recur everywhere in the *ukiyo-zōshi*. There is first of all the excess of vanity that leads to immodesty in dress and to a gaudy and expensive use of cosmetics ('Now young ladies smear it on down to their navels'); improper behaviour is another trend of the times ('A woman's morals nowadays are as changeable as a cat's eyes'), and its variations are practised by both young and old. Coquetry and wantonness abound. Rare indeed is the shy maiden who thinks of men only as terrifying creatures, blushes violently at the slightest touch, and, if anyone snatches at her sleeve or skirt, does not hesitate to scream . . .

But should a proper young lady behave otherwise?

Kiseki's regard for propriety seems somewhat literary, not to say theatrical. Even with this theme, obviously a sympathetic one, he weakens the severity of his sermon by a distracting sprightliness. And Saikaku can remain cheerful while observing the lower depths of female depravity. The bold heroine of *The Woman Who Spent Her Life in Love* often mentions the vanity of sensual pleasures; but though her highly coloured confessions run the entire gamut of harlotry, she seems scarcely more repentant, after all, than she did when her first affair ended with the execution of her secret lover, who then haunted her briefly:

It was so horrible I thought of killing myself. But the days passed and I forgot all about him. You know how shamefully fickle women are. Of course I was only thirteen at the time, so people were indulgent. Some of them said, 'Surely not at her age. . . .' That amused me.

She enjoys recalling how easily she seduced her employers during the few respectable interludes of her long life. There was the time when she took up writing love-letters for young men, so convincingly that she persuaded herself to fall in love with one of them. Later, a maidservant in a merchant's household, she upset the early morning Buddhist devotions of her master, and, as she remarks, made him forget all about Buddhism.

Still, Saikaku does not really seem to disapprove of her unusual tactics. Nor do his *Twenty Examples of Unfilial Conduct*—or Kiseki's *Characters of Worldly Young Men*—point a satisfactory moral. Genroku fiction seldom preaches without implying parody, and a bright satirical sketch is often enclosed in a thick Chinese border of Confucian moralizing. Even pornography followed this convention. Just as erotic *ukiyo-e* albums begin (and end) with sheets of irreproachable decency, only heightening the effects of what goes on in the other scenes, a thoroughly licentious *ukiyo-zōshi* may begin on a high moral plane, the

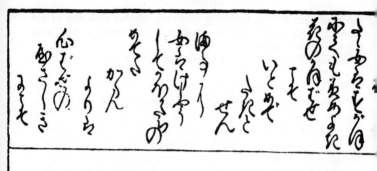

II. Moronobu: *One Hundred Women of Japan*

From right to left: a woman peers into a mirror on a lacquer stand as she carefully inserts a hairpin; another ties her sash; a third looks into a hand-mirror; the woman in a kimono with a stylized cloud pattern brushes on

lip-rouge; and the last, her right arm freed for action, vigorously combs her hair. The inscription at the top criticizes ladies who think only of dress, cosmetics, and coiffures. Instead of plastering on make-up and priding themselves on their good looks, they would do well to improve their dispositions.

descent from which gives the pleasing shock of burlesque. Partly, to be sure, the sermon was added out of deference to Government censors, so cursory in their reading that a banned book might be sold under another title. And partly, too, it was included because people still thought of didacticism as the chief aim of literature.

Most of Genroku popular prose had (or pretended to have) a didactic purpose. Among writers of superior birth there were many who sincerely wished to teach. The Confucianist Kaibara Ekken, for instance, adopting a plain style which must have been distasteful to him, wrote a number of books offering comprehensive rules of conduct. His advice was stringent. Here, for example, is one of his 'Thirteen Counsels' [16] to young ladies on the verge of marriage, which appeared a few years before Kiseki's more ample comment:

A woman must always take care to behave with the strictest propriety. She should get up early, go to bed at midnight, and, instead of napping, busy herself about the work of the house. Weaving, sewing, and spinning should not be neglected. She ought not to become addicted to tea or *sake*. Enjoying amorous songs or music is a special peril; she must avoid all improper amusements. As for shrines and temples, which are often visited for the wrong reasons, she will have plenty of time to go to them after the age of forty.[17]

Although Ekken was widely read throughout the Tokugawa Period, other writers imitated him at the expense of popularity. There was still a medieval tolerance of the creaking didactic framework, but the framework alone now seemed unpleasantly bare. And it might so easily be clothed. An unexceptionable moral could be illustrated by details that were not in themselves particularly edifying—details selected to show the deplorably gay, spendthrift city life of Genroku.

II

PLEASURES OF THE *UKIYO*

Among all the ways of enjoying the power of money none was safer, for the Genroku townsman, than to spend it on entertainment. In the gala world of actors, courtesans, and their attendant wits and sycophants, the wealthy rake found diversions to occupy a lifetime. A man who was not so well off could enjoy them as long as his money lasted, since anyone with a sense of style, and the means to support it, was welcome in this aristocracy. The many would-be rakes were also good customers for *ukiyo-e* and *ukiyo-zōshi*—so good that Saikaku, Kiseki, Moronobu, and the others could hardly have succeeded without an expert knowledge of *ukiyo* high life. But the Genroku popular artist had the entrée of these circles. Backstage, and at the tea-houses of the pleasure quarter, he saw the celebrities of the floating world at close range, in the intimacy of the green-room and the private banquet chamber. And he could sketch them, or describe them, with convincing detail.

This alone assured him some attention, for there was endless curiosity about actors and courtesans. Supposedly beneath contempt, they were in fact lionized everywhere, and expected to set the tone of *ukiyo* society. Even in early Genroku it was true (as Kiseki—and Saikaku—wrote) that ladies would 'ape the manner of harlots and courtesans, and of the actors who play female roles'. Most gentlemen were susceptible to that manner, and to the charms of the young men and women who assumed it. The two 'evil places', as those who disapproved of the theatre and the pleasure quarter called them, had become important social institutions.

Indeed, the vogue of the *ukiyo-zōshi* was mild in comparison with that of the Genroku theatre. If the *ukiyo-zōshi* depicted the world of pleasure, the theatre dominated it: new plays, innovations in scenery or costume, the private lives of the actors—these were engrossing subjects for discussion, and no one was so

23

blasé as to be indifferent to them. People of every rank, from shop-boys to samurai, were attracted by the colourful, day-long performances. Ladies of the Shogun's Court attended (in screened galleries), until it was learned that one of them had taken an actor as her lover. She, too, must have had a good deal of secret sympathy. Who could remain calm while a splendid warrior strode down the runway to enter battle, or held a breathless, contorted pose that revealed an agonizing conflict of loyalties? Many of the plays were superb spectacles, admir-ably designed to exalt the heroic actor. Such theatrical giants as Ichikawa Danjūrō I, the founder of the great line of Edo *kabuki* actors, swaggered more boldly than any Genroku samurai. Danjūrō and his rivals appeared in historical or pseudo-historical plays compounded of bombast, pageantry, choreographic sword-fighting, and noble dilemmas. But other actors, especially in Kyoto and Osaka, performed plays of a more realistic kind in which townsmen could see their own society, and be stirred by its problems of love and duty. Managers found that these modern domestic tragedies helped to fill their theatres. The plight of a shopkeeper infatuated with a courtesan, hopelessly in love but caught in a network of family and financial strains, seemed no less dramatic than the clash of sterner loyalties. And it was up to date. Yet the 'period pieces', too, had more than a dash of contemporary seasoning: not only were they full of anachronisms, often including a lively scene laid in the gay quarter, but some were based on recent struggles between members of the ruling class, brought to the stage under a thin Kamakura or Muromachi disguise.

As usual, the theatre was both an escape from life and a criticism of it. Even in the historical plays townsmen were not merely enchanted by hollow splendours and magnificent clap-trap. Behind the tableaux of old revenges, or quarrels between the feudal lords of another era, there were dreams of bravado, a show of forbidden ostentation, and not a few satirical comments on the Tokugawa samurai, their lords, and the Bakufu itself. The theatre offered a prismatic reflection of *ukiyo* fantasies, and coloured these images in turn. And they were vividly recorded in the *ukiyo-e* prints, of which huge quantities were used as advertisements and souvenirs. All the outstanding roles are illustrated in the gallery of actor prints. The heroic warriors of

Kiyonobu, drawn in the bold style of his trade as a painter of theatrical signboards, strike formidable attitudes, strangely unhampered by their two swords and many-layered garments. Their ferocity underlined by grotesque make-up, these and thousands of other fierce *ukiyo-e* figures delighted the townsmen. But besides the characters from historical drama there are still others, not so swaggering, from plays based on scandalous or tragic incidents of ordinary city life. Star-crossed lovers walk by on their way to suicide; the robber Gompachi, as played by Ichikawa Komazō, shares an umbrella with Komurasaki, a Yoshiwara girl who will kill herself after his execution; a hesitant beauty standing near a sedan chair holds a crucial letter. Many of the lovely women of the woodcut prints are in fact stage characters—played by men. *Onnagata*, the actors who specialize in such roles, appear most frequently as courtesans: arch, enticing, or demure, but always sinuously poised, they balance their heavy ornamental coiffures, bristling with combs and bodkins, and gracefully manœuvre the long sleeves and skirts of their flowered robes. Among these portraits are some of the most seductive, and the most richly dressed, of all the *ukiyo-e* beauties. One can imagine how the actors must have fascinated the townsmen, setting them ever higher standards of extravagance.

In the Genroku theatre sheer luxury of costume was much admired, except by the authorities. Now and then they would ban the use of fine silks and embroideries on the stage, or confiscate the expensive wardrobe of an actor. But sumptuary laws only added a spice to sumptuousness. The art of stage-setting, which had barely existed before Genroku, went on to more and more gorgeous effects: instead of the austere, unchanging pine at the back of the *nō* stage, the popular theatre had a variety of backdrops, and handsomely constructed sets showing forests, temple gates, palace courtyards, and whole street-scenes; instead of a slight, skeletal framework to represent a boat, there would be a full-scale junk on a billowing cloth sea. Sets were changed dozens of times in a day's performance—by late Genroku the desire for quick scene-shifting had led to the revolving stage, a device invented in Europe only at the end of the nineteenth century. Such refinements suggest the failure of Tokugawa propaganda for plain living and high thinking. Naturally there was also sporadic political and moral censorship of the plays them-selves, which were far too popular to escape suspicion. At times regulation was so severe that the stage seemed likely to be restricted to puppets.

For there were two kinds of popular theatre in Genroku: *jōruri* and *kabuki*, the puppet theatre and the theatre of human actors. Both had grown up in the course of the seventeenth century; each had influenced the other; and each (though they might seem unequal rivals) had found the other a dangerous competitor. The *jōruri*, named after Princess Jōruri, one of its early heroines, began as a kind of ballad-drama, chanted by wandering entertainers. Heroic narratives and popular Bud-dhist legends gave the reciters their material, and from these crude tales of gods, brave men, and vengeful demons came a new dramatic form of recitation. This was presented in alliance with a wonderfully expressive puppet theatre, to the accom-paniment of the 'three-stringed' *samisen*. The *samisen*, which had been introduced from the Ryūkyū Islands in the sixteenth century, was the favourite instrument of townsmen, for whom its dry, twanging notes evoked the atmosphere of the pleasure quarter. Visually, too, the *jōruri* theatre was irresistible. Its players were only hand-puppets, but, in their full Genroku development, two-thirds life-size and beautifully made. Many of them required the services of three men—a chief puppeteer, to move the head and right hand, and two assistants, for the left hand and feet. Eyes could be rolled by an inner mechanism, or a bushy eyebrow lifted. Yet such tricks were far less effective than their nuances of pose and gesture, coquettish or swashbuckling, and their remarkable dancing and sword-play. These compli-cated figures were manipulated so skilfully that Genroku actors —who also copied their costume, make-up, hair-dress, and borrowed voices—often mimicked their angular, stylized movements.[1]

Meanwhile the *kabuki* theatre, though remaining commercial, had evolved from an adjunct of prostitution to an art. The word *kabuki* itself was written euphemistically to mean 'the song and dance art', but in its original sense of 'lewdness' or 'abandon' it had been applied in early Tokugawa to troupes of women who allured men by singing, dancing, and performing humorous skits. Their stages were open-air platforms on the dry bed of the

Kamo River in Kyoto. Later real theatres were built, with increasingly complex equipment. Women were banned from the stage (possibly, in part, at the complaint of brothel-keepers); the dramatic literature was improved; and the great actor-dynasties, with their rigorous professional training, were established. By Genroku, after many vicissitudes, *kabuki* had become an artistic theatre. Its elements—dialogue, narrative recitation, song, dance, musical accompaniment, and all the other arts and crafts of the stage—were now combined in their classic form.

Much of this progress was due to the influence of the puppet theatre. For a time, especially in Kyoto and Osaka, *jōruri* overshadowed *kabuki*; it was not until the second half of the eighteenth century that *kabuki* began to outrival *jōruri* in Osaka, where the puppets had been most successful. The great dramatist Chikamatsu Monzaemon (1653–1725) spent the most brilliant part of his career in Osaka, as the permanent writer for a *jōruri* company. All his best plays were written for the puppet theatre—where the playwright was not subordinate to the actors. Chikamatsu refined and invigorated the Tokugawa drama, as Saikaku did its popular fiction; he gave it new psychological and poetic depth. But even Chikamatsu, who came from a samurai family, used incidents of *bourgeois* life—in particular the emotional entanglements of tradesmen—for some of his finest plays. And most of his domestic tragedies were built around the same extreme situation: a socially unacceptable romance culminating in *shinjū*, the double suicide of lovers. Often these plays were based on actual events, and written at top speed while they still had sensational appeal. This tragic theme so captivated the popular imagination that *shinjū* pieces were banned, to check an alarming increase in the number of love suicides.[2]

Whether or not the influence of the theatre could be fatal, it evidently permeated Genroku society. And it is significant that the *dénouement* of a Chikamatsu *shinjū* drama was usually the result of a love affair with a courtesan. Romance, rather than sex, was the forbidden fruit of the *yūkaku*, or 'pleasure quarter', but its temptations were hard to resist. Of course the more fashionable of these resorts were only for people who could afford expensive pleasures. Here, in a luxurious setting,

merchants and sufficiently prosperous samurai enjoyed sparkling, vivacious company, such as could be found nowhere else in
Japan. The chief pleasure quarters—the Shimabara in Kyoto,
the Edo Yoshiwara, and the Osaka Shimmachi—were made up
of large groups of buildings, some magnificent, which served
as the fine restaurants, the exclusive clubs, and the leading
salons of the day. Among them were great 'tea-houses' (as
brothels were often called), where famous courtesans came to
join the candle-lit banquets and parties given by men of
fashion. One such house, the Sumi-ya in the Shimabara, still
stands—and has been designated an Important Cultural
Property. Not only is this handsome establishment a spacious
one, from its reception hall to its vast kitchen, but it is also in
the best of taste: a delightful garden, polished corridors, sliding
panels decorated by the foremost painters, a distinctive screen
pattern and style of metal fittings for each room. The general
effect is chaste and aristocratic, rather than voluptuous or
rococo. Against this kind of background an essentially mere-
tricious social life was seen to peculiar advantage.

It is easy to imagine the fascination of the Genroku courtesans; for they bear a close family resemblance to their urbane
descendants in the familiar *ukiyo-e* prints of the later eighteenth
century. In the colour prints that the West has so much admired, many of them advertising women of the pleasure
quarter, the celebrities of the *ukiyo* are seen at ease in their
accustomed settings, apparently unaware of the artist's
presence. Kiyonaga's tall beauties, stately in the most casual
dress, cross the Sumida River to the Yoshiwara by ferry-boat,
or sit quietly enjoying the evening air. One fans herself list-
lessly; a companion, barefoot, wearing a striped pink summer
kimono, smokes a slender brass pipe as she leans against a
wooden balustrade. Scenes at the bath and in the boudoir illustrate the stages of preparing to entertain worldly men: a
woman who has stepped from the tub scrutinizes herself in a
round hand-mirror, while another, before a tiny dressing-table,
carefully paints her eyebrows. Courtesans of the upper class of
this feudal demimonde, escorted by servants and girls of lesser
rank, promenade through the narrow streets of their quarter
with regal dignity. And the attenuated, provocative women of
Utamaro exhibit a sinister adroitness in handling pipes, fans,

toys, and writing-brushes; for their charm, though refined to its quintessence, is not at all disinterested. The women of the 'green houses', whether in Genroku or a century later, possessed all the arts necessary to empty the purses of discriminating men.

To be sure, the great ladies of this society were simply the most privileged members of a hierarchy (its gradations accounted for by a large vocabulary) [3] which descended at last, outside the gay quarter, to street-walkers of the sort that haunted the Kamo bridges in Kyoto. A girl who had been apprenticed to this profession, bound by contract in return for a loan to her parents, might have the good fortune to be ransomed by a wealthy rake, as in Kiseki's 'Spendthrift'; or she might eventually become a teacher of dance and music, or a procuress. But she might very well end her career as miserably as Saikaku's heroine in *The Woman Who Spent Her Life in Love*. Still, the *grandes cocottes* were paid such homage that no one would have put them in the same category with women of the street. At the top of the hierarchy stood the *tayū*, courtesans of the highest rank: in 1702 (as a result of the excessive formalities required in meeting them) their number had dwindled until there were only four *tayū* among some two thousand women of the Yoshiwara. [4] Sumptuously gowned and ceremoniously attended, these rare beauties were proud, spirited women who selected their favourites with care and required of them an ardent courtship. The more famous ones are still remembered, and their lives are recorded in standard biographical dictionaries. But even courtesans of somewhat lower degree had to be exceptionally gifted and thoroughly trained. They were expected to be adept at poetry, calligraphy, music, and the tea ceremony—and at conversation, to which they brought a mastery of innuendo and the ability to match any man in sarcastic or *risqué* talk. In these impressive surroundings, with these fascinating women, men of the world found the glamour denied by Confucian propriety and a rigid family system.

It was in the scintillating company of the pleasure quarter, then, that *ukiyo* writers and artists could observe the reigning beauties of their day, and study the airs and affectations of the great rakes. For Genroku men of fashion cultivated an equally artificial manner. As Saikaku's worldly heroine points out, a gentleman was expected to dress in the height of style, to behave

III. Sukenobu: *Studies of One Hundred Women*

A *tayū* of the Kyoto Shimabara quarter leads the procession (from the right), attended by two courtesans of lesser rank, by a little apprentice, and by a

procuress who holds a long-handled umbrella. The pipe-smoking girl sitting on a high lacquer clog (worn on formal promenade) is a courtesan of the fourth rank.

with casual but correct nonchalance, and to drop suitable comments on music, the *nō* drama, and classical poetry ('Thus, beginning with two or three elegant remarks, he conducts himself suavely and with great composure'). Attended by clever *taiko-mochi* ('jesters', professional male entertainers and party companions), he would play his role as assiduously as any *kabuki* actor.

Men of this sort are often seen in the *ukiyo-e*. On a spring afternoon in Kyoto a dandy strolls along the river, his kimono black and crimson against pale green willows, his parasol tilted exquisitely; another, at a Gion tea-house, lies propped on one elbow near a tobacco tray and a small lacquer table, in a cluster of attentive courtesans, and listens indifferently as one of them sings to the accompaniment of her *samisen*; others relax on a veranda by a garden, or saunter through night streets led by girls with paper lanterns. Picnics, banquets, hot-spring visits, flower-viewing excursions, boating parties—all the amusements are represented, in an endless variety of scenes, and at each the young rakes are shown behaving with the nonchalance required by Tokugawa etiquette. Their languid manner is as stylized as their hair-dress, or the patterns of their garments. Yet these are not merely anonymous fashion-plates. Like the pictures of Genroku courtesans, they were identified with particular subjects—the principal actors, rakes, and dandies of the floating world.

People who would never meet these glamorous figures could enjoy their society vicariously—in the theatre, in the *ukiyo-e*, and in the *ukiyo-zōshi*. Popular art and literature reflected the Genroku obsession with the entertainments—and the entertainers—of the two 'evil places'. Genroku publishers were of course aware of this interest, and quite willing to supply their own entertainment of every saleable kind, from poetry to pornography. Besides issuing an immense number of woodcut prints, albums, and picture books, in which the more decorative aspects of theatre and pleasure-quarter life could be found, they published a variety of stories and sketches showing still other views, psychological or satirical, of that glittering world beyond the means of so many of their readers. Since the book had become an article of trade, the reading public was no longer exclusive: a haphazard commercial revolution had overthrown intellectual, if not social, barriers.

In early Tokugawa, however, printed books had been rarer than manuscripts, and it would have been difficult to imagine the extraordinary growth of seventeenth-century publishing. Type-printing had been introduced from Korea in the late sixteenth century; but this technique, which the Jesuits also brought to Japan at about the same time, was chiefly used for important works—histories, books of the Confucian canon, Chinese treatises on government or strategy—printed under the patronage of the Emperor or the Shogun. Soon, though, a few privately sponsored books were issued, most of them by the rich Kyoto connoisseur Suminokura Soan for presentation to his friends. These are the Saga-bon: *éditions de luxe* of Japanese poetry, *nō* plays, and masterpieces of Heian and medieval prose. Among them, for instance, is a 1608 edition of *The Tales of Ise*—edited by a scholar-poet of the Court nobility, illustrated in the Tosa style, and beautifully printed (with type designed by an expert calligrapher) on paper in five delicate tints.[5]

As commercial publishers began to appear, the classics were reprinted, extracted, or vulgarized, to suit a very different kind of reader. Kyoto, the centre of scholarship and the arts, became also the source of a flood of popular miscellanies, guidebooks, tales, and tracts. These are called *kana-zōshi*, or 'books in the vulgar script', and it is true that their primary aim was vulgarization. *Kana-zōshi* were the first books written expressly for townsmen, as well as the first printed for mass distribution. By the middle of the seventeenth century the ancient method of block-printing, familiar in Japan for nearly a thousand years, had superseded movable type. Wood-block editions were cheap, easy to illustrate, and convenient for reproducing a handsome, fluent script.[6] A best-selling *kana-zōshi* would be issued in several thousand copies—each of which (though there were no lending libraries before Genroku) must have had many readers.

Bookshops became as common as bath-houses. In 1626 there were already fifty in Osaka; and by Genroku, when *kana-zōshi* gave way to *ukiyo-zōshi*, the trade had expanded to include pedlars, like the walking bookstall in one of Shigenaga's prints, and even a few well-established businesses headed by owners of the second or third generation. Printing, publishing, and selling were carried on at the same shop, but circulation had been

33

increased by a tendency to specialize. A Kyoto house might deal in the texts of puppet plays, or in dramatic criticism; it might co-operate with other Kyoto booksellers, or with those in Osaka, or even Edo—still somewhat provincial. Saikaku's first novel (*The Man Who Spent His Life in Love*) was published in Osaka in 1682 and pirated in Edo two years later, but his *Twenty Examples of Unfilial Conduct* (1686) was published jointly in Osaka and Edo. Indeed, the Hachimonji-ya, for which Kiseki wrote, was such an enterprising and successful house that its name has become a generic term for the late Genroku *ukiyo-zōshi*. As profits increased, publishers competed briskly to introduce their authors to more and more readers. Fiction-writing became a possible, if degrading, means of livelihood.

The growth of this new reading public, which Saikaku and Kiseki helped recruit, was accelerated by the high rate of literacy among Genroku townsmen. As early as the *kana-zōshi* era the sons of ordinary city people could learn to read at temple schools—not that they were encouraged to read ephemeral fiction, or even the Heian classics. The education of townsmen, in the official view, had the sole purpose of informing them of their moral and social duties. And *kana-zōshi*, written by persons of higher rank, bore a heavy weight of precept and admonition.[7] If you preferred something more entertaining than homiletic dialogues, Buddhist cautionary tales, and Confucian conduct-books, you had very little choice: a bad popular version of *Genji*; an adaptation of queer Chinese stories of murder, or of ardent young women who were really foxes; a few pallid romantic tales continuing a feeble Muromachi strain. The favourite among these was *Urami-no-suke*,[8] a melancholy account of love and frustration in the upper classes; there was also *The Tale of Usuyuki* [9]—in epistolary form, useful as a model for letter-writing, but similar to *Urami-no-suke* in its plot and in its florid archaic style. Exotic or sermonizing or pseudo-aristocratic, all belonged to a world apart from that of the townsman. But the irreverent *ukiyo* spirit had begun to penetrate the *kana-zōshi*. It is symptomatic that the revival of interest in Heian literature took an erratic turn towards parody, and monuments of classical prose were reconstructed for humorous effect. Even the exquisite poetic sketches of *The Tales of Ise* were retold as *Tales of Nise* (that is, *Fake Tales*),[10] with the mood changed so that in

certain episodes, for instance, the pangs of hunger were substituted for those of love.

As the reading public grew larger, its dislike of dull or
patronizing books became more insistent. Authors and publishers responded to its demands, but hesitantly; and their
mixed aims gave the *kana-zōshi* a marked transitional character.
Practical information was set in a story framework, or carefully
embellished; moral teachings were interspersed with amusing
anecdotes; old-fashioned romantic tales were enhanced by
realistic touches. When these rather confused tendencies
coalesced, there emerged the genre that was later called the
ukiyo-zōshi. Here, in the books of Saikaku and his followers, the
people of the floating world discovered that stories of their own
antics and aberrations were as entertaining as any of the tales
imported from China, or handed down in their own country.
Fox-women, warriors, and princesses remained in literary
fashion; but they now seemed *too* familiar, in contrast with such
ukiyo figures as the dissolute young man, the accomplished
courtesan, or the wayward wife.

III

SAIKAKU

THE Man Who Spent His Life in Love,[1] an erotic picaresque novel of 1682, is the first of the more than two dozen books with which Ihara Saikaku, in a single decade, brought Genroku fiction to maturity. It is also the first *ukiyo-zōshi*. Indeed, Saikaku's brilliant novels, stories, and sketches define the genre —somewhat vaguely, we may feel, since they exhibit such variety. But if these and other *ukiyo-zōshi* seem to have little in common, except for the eccentricities to be discussed later, still their piquant flavour is easily recognized. Suiting as they do the special tastes of a narrow, homogeneous social group, they resemble *ukiyo-e* in the singularity and strength of their under-lying generic style. To be sure, each of Saikaku's most famous *ukiyo-zōshi* has a different structure: a long, eventful account of a rake's progress; a harlot's progress, told by the woman her-self; a set of five short tales of passionate women; a book of vivid sketches of merchant life, linked by theme and setting. And Kiseki's range from vignettes of typical *ukiyo* figures, of the kind here translated, to lengthy adaptations of *jōruri* and *kabuki* dramas. Yet all these *ukiyo-zōshi* have a characteristic manner, and imply (what had been rare since the Muromachi Period) an affinity between the writer of fiction and his readers. *Ukiyo-zōshi* evoked the atmosphere of the floating world, and echoed the sentiments of the Genroku townsman instead of those of his superiors, past or present. Doubtless many samurai enjoyed reading them—discreetly, just as their lords viewed *kabuki* per-formances from screened boxes. But townsmen were the new arbiters of taste, and they had become sensitive to the tone of condescending authors.

Saikaku expressed the opinions and predilections of his readers, though not uncritically. His stories have a tinge of cynicism, in refreshing contrast to the old platitudes about moonlight and cherry blossoms. 'People are not so fond of having plum, cherry, pine, and maple around the house', he observes, 'as gold and silver, rice and hard cash.' [2] But he shares the fundamental Genroku respect for money. His later books, in which business comes before pleasure, have its importance as their theme. In *The Everlasting Storehouse of Japan* [3] (1688) he sums it up with a passing reference to the latter-day aristocracy: 'Money is the townsman's pedigree, whatever his birth and lineage. No matter how splendid a man's ancestors, if he lacks money he is worse off than a monkey-showman.' [4] Cleverness and hard work are therefore the highest virtues of the towns-man, and the tales of *The Everlasting Storehouse* bear out its irreverent sub-title: *The New Bible for Getting Rich.*

Few traditional ideas go unquestioned by Saikaku. In *The Woman Who Spent Her Life in Love* [5] he argues, citing the much-poeticized view at Matsushima, that the beauties of nature have been greatly overrated. Elsewhere, one of his stories begins with the astonishing remark: 'I was so bored with cherry blossoms I stayed away from the capital all spring.' [6] Or, after pointing out that modern women are easily corrupted, Saikaku slyly adds: 'That, unfortunately, is what the morals of the lower classes have sunk to, but this sort of thing, of course, never ever happens among the upper classes.' [7] But the misbehaviour of townsmen was his chief interest, as it was his readers', and the fickle, greedy, light-hearted men and women he wrote about were in fact recognizable people of the *ukiyo.*

How fiction had changed may be seen by comparing one of Saikaku's stories with *Urami-no-suke*, the best of the early seventeenth-century romances. *Urami-no-suke* is the tale of an unhappy love affair which begins when the hero (named in the title) visits a temple with his friends and happens to catch sight of a beautiful young girl. She is a romantic cliché, set forth in antiquated conceits—her moth-eyebrows are 'like the moon in distant mountains'. 'What painter could achieve such loveliness with his brush? Even if I were to strain for comparisons'—and here the author lists a full page of beauties, from Yang Kuei-fei, the favourite of the Emperor Hsüan Tsung, to the numerous loves of Prince Genji—'how could any of these surpass her?' [8] Naturally Urami-no-suke is captivated, and after lengthy negotiations (with suitable go-betweens, in the genteel tradition of Heian literature) contrives to correspond with her. Thanks to the intervention of the goddess Kannon, he is able to visit her one night. But as time passes they have no further opportunity to meet. He begins to pine, and at last succumbs to love-sickness before another rendezvous can be arranged. Hearing this, the girl kills herself, and her confidantes commit suicide to follow her in death. Friends bury the lovers together.

Saikaku's stories are less sentimental, and more scandalous: those of *Five Women in Love* [9] (1686) are based on actual incidents of the time. In one, a young married woman falls into adultery quite by chance, and is at last executed with her lover at Awataguchi.[10] She, too, is beyond compare (at least within her neighbourhood), and has moon-shaped eyebrows like 'the crescent borne aloft during the Gion Festival parade'. But Saikaku remarks that there is no need to go into detail about such an evident beauty. And his heroine makes her first appearance in an ordinary Kyoto street, where a group of young blades are looking over the pretty girls. Some of them seem as lovely as *ukiyo-e* courtesans, but since they are not legendary creatures, they cannot be expected to be flawless. One of the more promising is described in this way:

Next they spied a lady of thirty-three or thirty-four with a long, graceful neck and intelligent-looking eyes, above which could be seen a natural hairline of rare beauty. Her nose, it was true, stood a little high, but that could easily be tolerated. Underneath she wore white satin; over that, light blue satin; and outside, reddish-yellow satin. Each of these garments was luxuriously lined with the same material. On her left sleeve was a hand-painted likeness of the Yoshida monk, along with this passage: 'To sit alone under a lamp, and read old books. . .'. [11] Assuredly, this was a woman of exquisite taste.

Her sash was of folded taffeta bearing a tile design. Around her head she had draped a veil like that worn by court ladies; she wore stockings of pale silk and sandals with triple-braided straps. She walked noiselessly and gracefully, moving her hips with a natural rhythm.

'What a prize for some lucky fellow!' one of the young bucks exclaimed. But these words were hardly uttered when the lady, speaking to an attendant, opened her mouth and disclosed that one of her lower teeth was missing, to the complete disillusionment of her admirers.[12]

Saikaku has the knack of deflating enthusiasm, and of placing his characters unmistakably in the setting of the *ukiyo*. For the first time townsmen could see themselves, in their intense pursuit of happiness, through the lens of artistic fiction.

Now, too, fiction was being created by men of their own sort. Genroku writers, though a group of skilled professionals, were neither influenced by aristocratic criticism nor isolated in cliques and coteries. Saikaku, like the others, belonged to the society for which he wrote, and in which he discovered his proper subject. And he belonged to its gayest set. Whether or not he came from a wealthy merchant family, as he probably did, Saikaku was a native of Osaka, knew the other great cities too, and was at home in the pleasure quarters of all of them. His tastes in literature were those of the sophisticated Genroku man of the world.[13]

Yet it may be noted that Saikaku, who lived from 1642 to 1693, was nearly an exact contemporary of the great and saintly poet Matsuo Bashō (1644–94), and also made his reputation as a writer of *haikai*—of the new, free style of linked-verse, that is, and of the derivative seventeen-syllable form now known as *haiku*. But their schools of *haikai*, and their temperaments, were not at all alike; two more divergent literary careers would be hard to find. While Bashō contemplated the doctrines of Zen Buddhism, or wandered on long, ascetic pilgrimages through the Japanese country-side, Saikaku broke all records by composing thousands of linked-verses in a single day—and did it without abandoning his pursuit of more worldly pleasures, and of the money needed to enjoy them. Besides turning to prose fiction, he tried his hand at *jōruri*—unfortunately in competition with Chikamatsu—and criticisms of *kabuki* actors. Again, with the usual Genroku versatility, he illustrated a number of his own *haikai* collections and books of fiction: his *ukiyo-zōshi* illustrations are highly regarded by many critics and connoisseurs. Needless to say, he was an expert calligrapher.

But it was in 1682, at the age of forty, that Saikaku began the major phase of his literary career. In that year he published his first novel, *The Man Who Spent His Life in Love*, and with it became at once the leading writer of Genroku popular prose. So successful was this venture that he continued to produce books of fiction, on an average of twice a year, for the rest of his life.

His earlier books are full of rakes and courtesans, and their strenuous fast-living, but as time went on he turned from erotic themes to the hard economic problems of the townsmen. Yet in all his *ukiyo-zōshi*, even those which use such traditional *kana-zōshi* themes as vendetta and the supernatural, Saikaku maintains an air of detached gaiety. Even episodes of despair and degradation are lighted up by flashes of wit. Saikaku knows the dark side of his world, and reminds us of it from time to time; but his technique is to interweave light and shadow. No one who has read *The Woman Who Spent Her Life in Love* can look at the butterfly elegance of *ukiyo-e* courtesans as if their beauty existed wholly apart from the poignant realities of the 'gay quarter'. Nor is it only in his later episodes that Saikaku suggests what bitterness lies ahead of even a first-rank courtesan, who 'without the slightest virtue can enjoy luxuries beyond the reach of the aristocracy'. Still, he takes a humorous view of life, bitter as it may be, and sees that his heroine, when she has joined the lowest street-walkers, is reminded that among *them* good looks would be superfluous, indeed wasteful, on a dark night. Saikaku's humour, though at times it appears to be unfeeling, is a useful literary stratagem. Mingling the comic with the serious, he creates a style of satirical, poetic realism with which he can depict both the pleasant and the unpleasant aspects of the floating world.

Saikaku and his followers brought a new range of experience to Japanese fiction. Also, since they chose to write about their own society, particularly its most colourful segment, they brought a new set of limitations. *Ukiyo* writers, belonging to the lower classes, were already narrowly hemmed in, if not yet to the satisfaction of the Bakufu. Social or political criticism was both futile and taboo: a too-pointed satire was a weapon that could easily be turned against its author. But perhaps their worst limitation—one that the tears and melancholy of earlier fiction leave us unprepared to find—was emotional. Most *ukiyo* writers adopted a rather flippant air. Their carefully worn attitude of brash nonchalance seems often to have been deliberately shallow, as if they hesitated to look beneath the attractive surface of *ukiyo* life. For Genroku townsmen, manners and forms had taken on special meaning, having grown more and more independent of the feelings. Detachment was cultivated in life as well as in art—and with some success. But the fact that this was one of the great ages of pornographic art has the same emotional implications as the curious brothel-salon society itself, suggesting how a repressive code, and the need for outlets of whatever kind, affected a volatile, responsive people. Erotic literature was also an escape. One senses, beneath its reckless wit and its often ridiculous sexual daring, a deep, unconscious reticence.

Yet these limitations, though severe, were not the artificial boundaries of the old romances. *Ukiyo-zōshi* writers treated significant new social types, people engaged in the exciting pursuit of money and pleasure. Having arrived in urban society, the *arrivistes* now invaded literature. Snobbishness and disdain for vulgarity were re-defined. Usurers, profiteers, actors, and courtesans supplanted the lofty figures of the tales of war and Court life. Martial, ascetic, or sentimental heroes were rejected in favour of heroic spendthrifts—men like the merchant Kinokuniya Bunzaemon, who is said to have had the staircase of a tea-house widened so that a huge pastry could be brought up to him. And modern heroines, usually of the demimonde, were not simply compared to the legendary perfection of Ono no Komachi or Yang Kuei-fei, but were described by going into such minutiae of costume and hair-dress that commentators find themselves engrossed in the study of Genroku customs. Misty landscapes became scenes of busy, shop-lined streets or, as so often in the *ukiyo-e* prints, of the glamorous theatre and pleasure quarters, where the twang of the *samisen* covered the discreet click of the abacus. Writers and print designers lived in a milieu from which, once technical innovations had discovered them, came a variety of themes and motifs for art.

Still, the most direct influence on an artist is the nature of his medium and the tradition of its use. Saikaku, as the chief innovator, was especially sensitive to convention, that 'necessary difference between art and life'.[14] His repertoire of devices is drawn from every level of Japanese literature, from the stock types and naïve story-telling methods of earlier folktales to the delicate ingenuities of classical poetry. He may borrow a convenient *deus ex machina* from Muromachi fiction, or take a figure from the common store of typical shrews, rustics, liars, drunkards, and the like. Even his piecemeal borrowings from the classics—from poetry, *nō* plays, Heian fiction—amount to a heavy debt; and it is not surprising, since he was among the foremost poets of his time, that he exploited poetic techniques in his prose rhythms and syntax, figures of speech, and quick associational transitions. Saikaku uses all the devices of Japanese poetry: 'pillow-words', 'pivot-words', ellipses, and the rest. He is especially fond of linking phrases by verbal associations (*engo*), to which he often gives an ironic flavour by juxtaposing the sublime and the ridiculous, the classical and the commonplace.

But augmenting the conventions of fiction from those of verse is itself conventional in Japan, where generic intermingling has always been the rule. Prose fiction began as a vehicle for poetry; the drama has consistently relied on third-person narration; lyricism has pervaded both drama and fiction. And Saikaku produced his first *ukiyo-zōshi*, *The Man Who Spent His Life in Love*, by adapting the kaleidoscopic *haikai* style to the manner of the travel guide and the Yoshiwara or Shimabara handbook. As often happens, prose forms meant to serve another purpose had been drawn into the vortex of imaginative fiction. The methods of the popular *kana-zōshi* guidebooks, which were necessarily realistic, led Saikaku to the genre of the erotic picaresque, a kind of fiction that was close to *ukiyo* life. Fragmentary views of that life are recomposed imaginatively in his novel. From one brief scene to another, in a *haikai*-sequence of sharp, fleeting images, an extraordinary daydream takes concrete shape.

In *The Man Who Spent His Life in Love* Saikaku surveys a rake's progress from precocious childhood to lecherous old age. We follow the career of the indefatigable Yonosuke through juvenile delinquency, disinheritance, and years of wandering, and his palmy days as a complete man about town—the convenient death of his father having made him rich. Yonosuke, the ideal Genroku amorist, outdoes even Prince Genji (his Heian counterpart) in his single-minded pursuit of love. Only, Yonosuke's experiences in the Genroku pleasure resorts make up a fantastic Baedeker of brothels, compiled from the very latest information. Burlesquing *The Tale of Genji* adds to the amusement of these absurd feats of profligacy. For example, there is a distant allusion to the famous 'rainy night's talk' in which Genji and his friends discuss the various kinds of ladies who might conceivably interest them (' "As for the lower classes, they do not concern us" '): [15] Yonosuke and his fellow-rakes, out boating one afternoon, while away the time by comparing the charms of the leading courtesans. But their debate soon leads to action. They agree that Yūgiri, a girl of the Osaka Shimmachi, is utterly incomparable—and Yonosuke, pretending illness, leaves the party early to go home and write her a persuasive love-letter. By the end of the chapter she has become one of the 3,742 women in his life.[16] Most of the other episodes are as concise, and as free from Heian restraint. Then in the last pages of the novel, after this incredible career of dissipation, Yonosuke turns philosophical at the age of sixty: 'I've been around every one of the pleasure quarters in this wide world, till I find I'm quite emaciated by love; and now at last the floating world has lost all attraction for me. . . .' [17] Whereupon he sails off to seek the fabulous Island of Women.[18]

A very different end awaits the heroine of Saikaku's other great erotic picaresque novel: *The Woman Who Spent Her Life in Love* (1686). Although she is like Yonosuke in her remarkable zest for life, her equally active career follows a steep downhill course. She begins with all the advantages except wealth: superb culture, thanks to a connexion at Court, and matchless beauty of face and figure. She exceeds even the requirements of a fastidious feudal lord—yet that affair turns out badly, as do all the others. Misfortunes mark each change of bedfellows. After a succession of brilliant failures as Court attendant, dancing girl, concubine of a provincial lord, and courtesan of the highest rank, she sinks through the lower ranks of the licensed quarter, leaves for a taxing stay at a monastery, becomes a professional letter-writer (specializing in love-letters), and goes on from one dubious trade to another. Among them are those of the vagrant psalm-singer (and harlot), tea-house girl, bath girl, shopkeeper's decoy, unlicensed prostitute, procuress, and at last street-walker. The few humdrum interludes are brief. Easily bored with any respectable occupation, particularly that of housewife, Saikaku's heroine can only turn to the more degrading varieties of prostitution. As her beauty fades, her income necessarily declines. And the end of the novel is implicit in its beginning, since it has been told retrospectively through her memories of 'all the many passions and vicissitudes of her life'. These are the confessions of a withered crone who has finally realized the evils of sensuality—for which in any case she is now far too old.

Perhaps *The Woman Who Spent Her Life in Love* treats *ukiyo* debauchery more critically than any other Genroku novel. The last of Saikaku's full-scale novels of passion, it may easily be contrasted with the first—*The Man Who Spent His Life in Love*. But there are many similarities. Both, for example, include a strong element of burlesque: the story told by Saikaku's heroine has a very different tone from that of the true Buddhist confessional tale, in which worldly vanities are renounced with some conviction.[19] *The Woman Who Spent Her Life in Love* is at once a highly accelerated harlot's progress and an entertaining tour of the entire Genroku demimonde. Saikaku's cheerful cynicism accepts the sordid as well as the attractive, and his inexhaustible vitality carries off scenes of whatever kind. Nothing is too bawdy, or too banal, for his vigorous art. Like Moronobu's *ukiyo-e*, Saikaku's *ukiyo-zōshi* mirror the bewildering variety of the floating world.

Both Saikaku and Moronobu achieve their finest effects by sheer stylistic verve; neither restricts himself to the obviously decorative. In the picture book *One Hundred Women of Japan*[20] (1695) Moronobu shows a number of handsomely dressed ladies at leisure—but along with others, not so elegant, who are sewing, washing, weaving, spinning, rice-planting, or gathering salt. The diversity of life—the many ways of making a living—delights him. In his *Pictures of Japanese Occupations*,[21] which was issued in 1685, we see priests, physicians, wrestlers, fortune-tellers, dancers, blind musicians, women of the street, artisans of all kinds, pedlars of clams, fish, rice cakes, bean curd, and pots and pans. A set of 'occupations of Japan' was a traditional subject, in painting and in poetry, but Moronobu has given it the fresh realistic detail of contemporary city life. Clam-pedlars and fishmongers do not cut such a dash as samurai, rakes, or courtesans. Still, they have their particular dress, their mannerisms, their comic shrewdness. And they are part of the endlessly changing Edo street scene, in which Moronobu takes so much pleasure.

Saikaku, too, enjoys the complexity of city life. And not only of demimondaine life: in 1686, less than half a year after the appearance of *The Woman Who Spent Her Life in Love*, he completed a group of presumably didactic stories called *Twenty Examples of Unfilial Conduct in Japan*.[22] In these he had withdrawn, perhaps under official pressure, from the less edifying environment of the gay quarter, and had begun to explore the themes of fortune and success which were to be developed in his later sketches of the floating world. His book is dedicated to 'the advancement of Filial Piety'—the prime virtue in the Confucian cult of the family, and one of the strongest themes of Japanese literature from the Heian 'step-child tale' to the modern newspaper serial. But Saikaku is an unconvincing moralist, even on this potent subject, and the title itself hints at parody. His readers were only too familiar with the Chinese *Twenty-four Examples of Filial Conduct*[23]—with Wang Hsiang, who had melted river ice by lying down naked on it, to bring his stepmother carp out of season, or with Meng Tsung, who had searched a snowy thicket for early bamboo shoots. Times had changed and these legends were obsolete. Saikaku dismisses them in the first words of his preface: 'Bamboo shoots in snowtime may be had at the greengrocer's; there are always live carp in the fishmonger's tanks.'[24] He intends, rather, to show the flagrantly unfilial conduct of his own day; and the opening passage of his first story makes it clear that the setting will be neither China nor the utopia of the Shogun's dreams, but the quotidian world of business and pleasure—a world where everything has its price:

Many are the ways of making a living. . . . Some spend the whole year painting paper banners of Benkei on the Gojō Bridge, with his seven pieces of arms and armour.[25] Some wander empty-handed through night streets where there may be an anxious parent,[26] and profess to cure disease by extracting worms through the fingertips. A man may carry a plane about, and offer to smooth down chopping-blocks (large or small) for three *mon*[27] each. You can rent what you need for a Buddhist service—sacrificial food, flower-vase, candlestick, censer, and a gong as well—all for twelve *mon* a night. A lying-in room couch, including the large pillow, will cost you seven *fun* a week. At the season for making rice cakes they rent steamers for three *fun* a day and two a night. Medicine pots are ten *mon* a week. If you want a large ditch cleaned, there are men who will do it for a *mon* every six feet, and will bring their own bamboo

IV. Moronobu: *Pictures of Japanese Occupations*

As their wary customers leave, the fishmonger cries 'Fresh fish!' and the
bearded clam-pedlar boasts of the beardlessness of his clams. Still, one man

looks narrowly over his shoulder at the clams; the other, in the basket hat,
seems to wonder if those 'live carp' in the tank are really swimming. Above
are two pairs of humorous verses (with notes) on these useful occupations.

rakes and brooms, and dustbins too. Some go about with pruning shears, and will trim any tree for five *fun*, or make grafts at one *fun* a branch. A carpenter will do an odd job for six *fun*. A tub of hot bath-water will be delivered for six *mon*. Some make a summer business of renting bamboo-shades, through which you can easily glimpse the intentions of these clever fellows—let the thrifty housewife beware! Surely anyone who exerts himself in the slightest, and doesn't only idle away his time, can be certain to make a decent living.[28]

The *fun*, a small unit of silver money, was worth about seven *mon*, or copper cash; and these, together with such precious coins as the gold *ryō* (equal to several thousand coppers), had become the real measures of value, though samurai were supposed to hold them in contempt. The gold, silver, and copper coins scattered liberally throughout Saikaku's fiction are emblematic of a highly developed money economy. In a later story he comments on its penetration into remote mountain districts 'where they think dried fish grow on trees, and where no one would know what to do with an umbrella'.[29] But it was only in the city that men could earn a livelihood by painting banners for a single holiday, or by profiting from a small stock-in-trade. After glancing at these clever ways of 'making a living' (a theme unknown to courtly or military fiction), Saikaku examines a still cleverer one, as he introduces a Kyoto moneylender who makes secret loans to the sons of wealthy merchants. The terms are 'double on death'—agreement to repay twice the principal (within three days after the inheritance), plus brokerage fees, interest, and miscellaneous charges. On the whole, Saikaku seems less disturbed by filial ingratitude than by gullibility, and the virtues he emphasizes are utilitarian ones.

Though far from staid, Saikaku is irrepressibly *bourgeois*. He conducts his reader through the business and amusement quarters of Kyoto, but not to its venerable palaces and temples. A panoramic view of the city, its encircling hills, and its neat chessboard pattern of gardens, courtyards, and low-pitched grey roofs does not detain him. He turns at once to the life of its ordinary shops, houses, and dusty streets. To be sure, the long, crowded streets of Kyoto impressed even Kaempfer, who visited the city a few years later: 'Being at one end of a great street, it is impossible to reach the other with the eye, because of their extraordinary length, the dust, and the multitude of people they are daily crowded with.' [30] And the winding streets of Edo or Osaka were no less crowded.

Evidently Saikaku found all this exhilarating. But he cannot treat any subject, however prosaic, in a sober guide-book style. His prose is always intense, erratic, and concise. And its close texture is further enriched by historical and literary allusion— to the 'night streets where there may be an anxious parent', for example, recalling a well-known poem from a tenth-century Imperial anthology.[31] In his exuberant sentences he freely mingles literary expressions with fresh—and to the traditional-ist extremely vulgar—colloquialisms. Purists of his day found this mixture a violent literary cocktail. Even Kiseki, who liked it, seldom used Saikaku's phrases without diluting them to blend with his own simpler prose.

But none of the *ukiyo-zōshi* writers adopted a thoroughly realistic technique. They filled the rather conventional outlines of their fiction with jokes, bits of dialogue, literary fragments, fragmentary descriptions of the people of the floating world. Such writers as Saikaku and Kiseki are realists who yet accept much of the Japanese aesthetic tradition. And they lived in an age of woodcuts—not three-dimensional movies, nor even daguerreotypes. In all their fiction the familiar elements of the Genroku scene are shaped into patterns that have their own pleasing familiarity, like the formal calligraphic curves of the gowns of *ukiyo-e* courtesans.

~~~ IV ~~~

KISEKI AND THE HACHIMONJI-YA

EJIMA KISEKI[1] was born in 1667, a generation after Saikaku. As the son of a well-to-do Kyoto shopkeeper, he could afford to enjoy the pleasures and vices of the capital, and these he later turned to account as literary materials. His favourite character—the wastrel, the spoiled 'young master'—was a natural choice. There is a note of ironic sympathy in his sketches of the type:

Disdainful of the family trade ('How vulgar!'), he occupies himself with the various arts, and with voluptuous pleasures; debauchery becomes his chief pursuit. This, he feels certain, is the proper life for a man of wealth. Never thinking to mend his ways, he exhausts his patrimony in amusements which are beyond his means. Yesterday the master of sycophants, today their laughing-stock—and as he grows older he suffers actual hardships.[2]

Kiseki's own family fortune had been built up by his father and grandfather, successful rice-cake dealers, but it was too small to survive his early extravagance. The few facts known of his life recall his fictional accounts of the rake's progress. Having learned from experience how quickly a family's assets could dwindle away, he might have been expected to take a serious view of this theme. To be sure, his first character-book opens with the proverb 'A father slaves, his son idles, and the grandson begs'; and he frequently draws on the prudent wisdom embodied in other proverbs ('Talk of next year and the demons smile'). But Kiseki's fiction reflects the typical psychology of the Tokugawa popular writer. Gloomy thoughts could be dispelled by the fugitive pleasures of the floating world, and these pleasures are hotly pursued in his *ukiyo-zōshi*. A favourite scene is the extravagant party: men carousing at a tea-house, or a spa (where they give new headaches to people who have really come for the cure). In his sketches, the joys of the *ukiyo* are seldom clouded by problems outside the theatre and the pleasure quarter. Such amusements might lead to ruin, but it would be a pity—and in bad taste—to let thoughts of bankruptcy spoil the delightful progress towards it.

Kiseki spent his own youth in cultivating the expensive airs of a man of the world. At last, pressed for money, he reluctantly began to write for a living. Near the end of the seventeenth century he wrote a few texts for Matsumoto Jidayū, a *jōruri*-reciter then popular in Kyoto. Apparently Kiseki's *jōruri* had a cool reception, but they brought him to the attention of Andō Jishō (1662?–1745), who published at least one of them. Jishō (the second Hachizaemon) had succeeded his father as proprietor of the Hachimonji-ya, or Figure-of-Eight Shop, soon the most famous publishing and bookselling house in Japan. He had already shown his acuteness by being among the earliest—if not the first—to issue the scenario-like texts of *kabuki* plays. These (including several by Chikamatsu) he added to the Hachimonji-ya's usual line of books, to the *jōruri* in which it had specialized since emerging from mid-century obscurity.[3]

Within a few decades the Hachimonji-ya became the foremost shop of its kind. This was partly because of another new undertaking by Jishō: in 1699, having meanwhile hired Kiseki as ghost writer, he published *The Actor's Vocal Samisen*,[4] a book of lively comment (as the title implies) on the leading *kabuki* players of the season. It was the first of the Hachimonji-ya's many 'actor-critiques' [5]—a kind of handbook that had begun as a Rake's Guide to the more attractive youthful performers, but had gradually developed, with rising standards of *kabuki* technique, into a mixture of theatrical gossip and dramatic criticism. The *Vocal Samisen* was in three parts (one for each of the 'three cities'), each headed by a catalogue listing actors according to type of role and degree of skill. This was followed by individual appreciations of the actors. The rankings and critical observations of the *Vocal Samisen* echoed those of its predecessors, but what set it above all of them was its engaging style and—as the Genroku public was quick to notice—its physical merits: the wide, pleasing format, the fine mulberry paper, the careful engraving and printing, the calligraphy, and, in particular, the illustrations.

Here, the illustrator was Nishikawa Sukenobu, who seems to have been hired by Jishō at about this time. Sukenobu contributed a great deal to the success of the Hachimonji-ya, though, like Kiseki, he began his career by working for it as an anonymous employee. Later he became the leading *ukiyo-e* painter of his day, and the designer of many superb picturebooks. In these one finds a fuller poetic evocation of the life of the floating world than in the work of any other *ukiyo-e* artist. But even Sukenobu's *ukiyo-zōshi* illustrations, which he did not sign, reveal his extraordinary facility and grace. This polish, in some degree characteristic of all Hachimonji-ya books, made the *Vocal Samisen* appealing to Genroku connoisseurs.

No doubt Jishō paid especial attention to the quality of the illustrations, since a book without them, or with inferior ones, was unlikely to succeed. But he must also have been anxious to give his first actor-critique some literary interest, and this Kiseki did for him by prefacing each section with a dialogue on the theatre. In one, for example, Kiseki traces the origin of the Hachimonji-ya's first actor-critique to a rainy spring day's conversation between a physician, a worldly priest, and a man about town who 'talks theatre from morning to night' and 'has neither wife nor wit, but only too much money'.[6] These prefaces were more interesting than the criticisms themselves. One was reprinted as an *ukiyo-zōshi* piece; now and then others from later critiques were collected and issued separately.

The Actor's Vocal Samisen established a pattern for the critiques of other houses, as well as for those the Hachimonji-ya published regularly thereafter. Kiseki was sought out by competitors, lured away for a time, and then recovered by Jishō, who again wanted to expand his publishing activities. These plans were realized in 1701, when the Hachimonji-ya's first *ukiyo-zōshi* appeared. From Kiseki's brush, but unsigned, it was called *The Courtesan's Amorous Samisen*.[7] Readers tempted by this suggestion of worldly gaiety found the preface—with its seductive references to the songs and courtesans of the three great pleasure quarters—still more enticing. And perhaps not only townsmen. Tsunayoshi is said to have had a love affair with a Yoshiwara girl before he became Shogun; and the Emperor himself, according to the diary of a Genroku official, had a suspicious familiarity with the ballads of the Shimabara quarter, which had long been the undisputed centre of attraction in the capital ('. . . His Highness sings what are called fling-tunes! These are licentious songs . . . extremely improper . . .').[8] But to quote Kiseki's preface:

> Even the much-praised song of the nightingale at plum time cannot give such pleasure as the Shimabara fling-tune, the Yoshiwara following-tune, or the Shimmachi gate-tune. Whenever you hear them your heart is stirred. And the singer, with her charming face turned slightly away, her crimson tongue quivering—this is a picture to surpass all the beauties of moon, snow, blossoms, and autumn foliage. Truly, so long as life itself goes on, these ties should not be severed. How can there be any joy beyond them! Here, then, are the many beguilements of these irresistible women—the Edo *sancha* [9] beating the drum for love, the Kyoto *hikifune* and the Osaka *shika* singing and plucking the strings of love—all under the title of *Amorous Samisen*.[10]

Kiseki's readers were not disappointed. His book raised the price of paper, in the usual expression; for it soon had to be reprinted.

The stories and sketches in the *Amorous Samisen* were arranged after the manner of a 'courtesan-critique' [11]—a kind of handbook similar to the actor-critique, which had perhaps stemmed from it. Twenty-four in all, they were in five groups (one each for the pleasure quarters of Kyoto, Osaka, Edo, provincial towns, and ports); their heroines were among the courtesans whose names, along with ranks, fees, and other practical information, appeared at the beginning of each group. In the *Amorous Samisen*, however, this guide-book paraphernalia merely embellished a set of tales of the floating world. Besides following Saikaku in adopting the manner of the courtesan-critique, Kiseki adopted its very form—and thus implied that his stories were based on fact. Whether or not they were, they satisfied a familiar literary taste. Among their characters are such standard types as the ransomed courtesan, the faithful harlot, the disowned son, and the clever man ruined by love. Kiseki adds new touches here and there (a father is smuggled into his son's brothel in a *sake*-barrel), but he chiefly retells old anecdotes with his own kind of stylistic zest. It was this that made the *Amorous Samisen* so popular.

V. *Studies of One Hundred Women*

On the right, an apprentice-courtesan offers tea to the mistress of the house
as another practises calligraphy; on the left, a third plays the *samisen*. All

three little girls wear the typical striped sash, tied at the back. The two young women at their toilet are third- and fourth-rank courtesans.

And Jishō had done more than give his new writer another perennially favourite Genroku subject. He had also produced another handsome book, again with illustrations by Sukenobu. So great was its success that Sukenobu went on to do a number of picture-books of his own, most of these, too, celebrating the women of the pleasure quarter. In his *Studies of One Hundred Women*,[12] published by the Hachimonji-ya in 1723, he devoted his first volume to a succession of respectable women, from Empress and Court ladies to firewood-sellers and peasant wives, but gave the second up almost entirely to courtesans of the three cities, and of all ranks. Here the *tayū*, queen of the Kyoto Shimabara, occupies the place of honour in the hierarchy; below her come the leading courtesans of Edo and Osaka, followed by the Edo *sancha*, the Kyoto *hikifune*, the Osaka *shika*, and so on, down to a final trio of street-walkers, stopping by a tea-stall in the evening. Again, as in Moronobu, we are given intimate glimpses of women applying lip-rouge and tying up their hair. But Sukenobu's *One Hundred Women*, besides including many more figures than the earlier *One Hundred Women of Japan*, includes many more social types—each of them fluently drawn and conveniently labelled. In a sense, this is what Kiseki did, seeking to impart new life to a genre which had somewhat languished since the days of Saikaku. For the vogue created by *The Man Who Spent His Life in Love*, and by Saikaku's later fiction, had not been sustained by writers who, lacking his wit, dashed off stories that were merely derivative. *Ukiyo-zōshi* were slowly going out of fashion when, with his refreshing style, Kiseki gave the genre a new vitality.

The Courtesan's Amorous Samisen began a long series of what were then called 'courtesan-' or 'samisen-books'. Most of their titles include one or another of these insinuating words (*The Courtesan's Eggnog*,[13] *Elegant Samisen Virtuosities*),[14] or both (*The Courtesan's Companion Samisen*).[15] Of course flippant titles of this sort were intended merely to catch the reader's eye, and to suggest in a very general way what kind of book he might expect. Tokugawa fiction is notorious among bibliographers for its odd, whimsical titles, often made up (as race-horses are named) by using old ones in combined or slightly altered form, to make a play on words or to indicate a lineage. The Hachimonji-ya's pedigree was soon recognized as the most distinguished in its field. For a decade Kiseki faithfully exploited it: besides continuing to turn out actor-critiques regularly, he wrote more and more *ukiyo-zōshi*—sometimes several a year. In these he replaced the framework of the courtesan-critique— its catalogues and symmetrical arrangement by pleasure quarter—with other devices.

For example, *Elegant Samisen Virtuosities* (1706) recalls the confessional form of *The Woman Who Spent Her Life in Love*. But Kiseki uses it as a new setting for three stories of a sort seen often enough in Genroku fiction. These are told to a Kyoto rake and his party by a decrepit ex-courtesan—and by the old man, once an effeminate *kabuki* youth, with whom she now shares a house. In this way the visitors are able to compare two very different views of the life of pleasure.

Each of Kiseki's later *ukiyo-zōshi* has an element of scandalous wit. His greatest success was *Courtesans Forbidden to Lose Temper* [16] (1711), which won especial favour for its impudent parody of the Buddhist sermon style. There are sermonizing stories to illustrate the virtues of courtesans, along with controversies, in theological terms, about whether they make better lovers than *kabuki* young men. Yet such mock-religious frivolity was probably not very shocking: Buddhist parody had become so conventional, both in *ukiyo* art and literature, that it had to be given an audacious turn. This Kiseki did. By indulging the Genroku predilection for wit and novelty, he further strengthened the Hachimonji-ya's position.

Jishō, besides capturing most of the actor-critique trade, became the leading publisher of *ukiyo-zōshi*. But there were others active enough to challenge him for a time. In Osaka, Nishizawa Ippū (1665–1731) published as many as three of his own books in a single year. Ippū, an inventive writer, but particularly skilful at adapting plays and old military tales, was Kiseki's chief competitor as heir to Saikaku. None, however, was credited with more than a share of Saikaku's excellences. A critic writes:

Most of them tried to 'paint a tiger', and ended with a lap dog. Kiseki alone was able to achieve a striped cat. Frankly, even Ippū could do no better than a paper tiger, and there were many who copied the striped cat with the hope of representing a splendid fierce beast of the jungle.[17]

Yet Kiseki was not so well known as his lesser contemporaries. At first he had insisted on anonymity, to keep his standing as a gentleman of leisure; later, persuaded that a name would help to sell his books, he allowed Jishō to sign them. But Jishō played the part of author with undue relish and, what was still more annoying, refused to share the growing profits. Kiseki then tried the stratagem of opening his own shop, the Ejima-ya, possibly in response to the flattery of rival publishers. He proposed to co-operate with the Hachimonji-ya, but Jishō refused. Finally, in 1712, all relations were broken off, and Kiseki began to publish *ukiyo-zōshi* independently. In the preface to the earliest of them he told how Jishō had falsely signed his name to the Hachimonji-ya books; Jishō replied by calling him an impostor; and Kiseki, in the Ejima-ya's first critique (1714), explained his position fully and advised his readers not to be taken in by shoddy wares. 'The Hachimonji-ya publishes crow', he warned, 'and calls it heron.' [18]

Jishō's arguments were weak, though abusive; but he traded on the Hachimonji-ya's reputation by issuing works of his own, or by a new ghost writer, in the intervals between publishing his remaining Kiseki manuscripts. Other dealers joined forces with the Ejima-ya, hoping to divide and conquer, but even their aid failed to make it a success. Seven lean years later Jishō and Kiseki resumed their association, this time on an equal footing. The event was announced in 1719, with what another critic fond of beast imagery describes as 'the tantalizing reserve of a pair of deceitful badgers'.[19] Now both names were famous, and both were used; while the actual writing was probably often done by new employees under Kiseki's supervision. Most of the Hachimonji-ya books of this period are tedious *jōruri* and *kabuki* adaptations, some compounded of several plays to satisfy a growing taste for intricacies of plot.

Kiseki died in 1736, nearly twenty years after the reconciliation. Although his long-drawn-out quarrel with Jishō may never lack its page in literary history, his reputation has suffered from its inevitable link to the celebrated names of Jishō and Saikaku —names which, in regard to Kiseki, imply bad business and derivative art. But Kiseki was more than a hack-writer. He skilfully modified Saikaku's elliptical style, which could be embarrassingly opaque, and at the same time proved himself fertile in literary ideas. Of course he had the usual Genroku nonchalance about sources. If his admiration for Saikaku sometimes borders on larceny, even his near-pastiches are a nice blend of Saikaku's sparkling phrases and his own comparatively subdued prose. He candidly acknowledged this debt, which scholars are still busy calculating, yet probably incurred much of it by unconscious imitation. Certainly he went to Saikaku as a faithful disciple, anxious to emulate his master. Nevertheless, his gifts are of a different order; even the surface of his fiction does not really mirror Saikaku's.

His prose glides easily along, everything in its proper place, as he develops his narrative minutely, proceeding smoothly from one point to the next. It is entirely unlike the capricious and suggestive manner of Saikaku. Though he cannot match the latter's marvellous originality and brilliance, he surpasses him in his skill at the detailed rendering of a subject in its various aspects.[20]

The translator (whether into modern Japanese or a foreign language) can scarcely help effacing most of the differences between these two styles, both of which may seem bizarre to the modern reader. Even so, Kiseki's is a rather pale shadow of his master's.

Also it must be admitted that his chief innovation—the 'character-books' [21] in which he satirized particular sets of figures of the floating world—had been anticipated by Saikaku's *Twenty Examples of Unfilial Conduct*. Indeed, there had been other burlesques of Confucian didacticism still earlier, among the *kana-zōshi*. Kiseki's new *ukiyo-zōshi* style, which he devised shortly after leaving the Hachimonji-ya, was merely a more systematic perversion of the Confucian manner. Trying to out-manœuvre Jishō in business, he hit on the notion of deliberately writing a group of satirical *ukiyo-zōshi* sketches on a specific social type. The success of one such book led him to write others. And his books, which incidentally exhausted the more rewarding types, set an example that was followed by later writers for the rest of the eighteenth century. Thus a good deal of Tokugawa fiction was written under the influence of Kiseki's character-books.

Characters of Worldly Young Men,[22] the first and best of these, was published at the Ejima-ya in 1715. Its fifteen Characters, twelve of them illustrated, were divided among five slim fascicles. The preface declares that the author's purpose is severely moral, but hints—what the illustrations make clear—that his subject requires him to exhibit an alluring variety of misbehaviour. He begins by deploring the modern loss of virtue:

It was the rule in ancient times that a boy should undertake the Lesser Learning at eight and the Higher Learning at fifteen. But children of our day clench pipes in their teeth at eight, and at fifteen they scheme to ransom courtesans by borrowing against their inheritances. This they believe to be proper masculine conduct.

After sketching the rake's progress, with its miserable end, Kiseki explains that such error derives from violation of the rule of Filial Piety:

A father behaves with the utmost solicitude toward his son, and works up a lather earning money to supply him. But the son looks down on his 'boorish' father. 'Being so strict won't get you anywhere these days', he complains. 'I don't know what to do with him. I've warned him time and again, but he's like all the others—too stubborn to reform.'

Gathering together from far and wide an assortment of these singular 'Characters of Worldly Young Men', I have set them down under that title, and had my work carved directly on printing-blocks. May it aid in the advancement of Filial Piety! [23]

The last sentence occurs also in Saikaku's preface to *Twenty Examples of Unfilial Conduct*, of which the first story illustrates 'borrowing against their inheritances' ('double on death').[24] Kiseki, too, is concerned with unfilial sons and their foolish fathers, and his first Character imparts a suitable moral, in generalized terms. But when he goes on, after this pious window-dressing, and introduces particular young men in particular situations, he betrays a different attitude towards unfilial sons. In general, they make up a lively, diverting group. They engage in a picture-book collection of amusements and occupations. Some are engrossed in wrestling, or infatuated with courtesans—or perhaps excessively fond of writing poetry. Others, strangely, resemble in burlesque fashion their most dignified and respectable elders: the sons of shopkeepers aspire to be doctors, priests, or samurai. Often the results of their activities are quite unexpected—and unlikely to advance Filial Piety.

In fact, Kiseki himself disobeys the moralist's rule of *kanzen-chōaku* ('reward virtue and punish vice'). Virtue does not always triumph: studiousness and piety degenerate into arrogance and debauchery; an Edo *kabuki* costumier disowns his son for being *too* frugal ('The first thing of its kind since the Emperor Jimmu!').[25] More often, vice remains unpunished: a prodigious liar flourishes; the spendthrift son of a money-changer manages to dupe his father nicely. Again, the Character of a would-be samurai tells the success story of a disobedient, thoroughly unfilial son (' "You can't tell what bloody deed he may do tomorrow, to put a noose around his old father's neck!" '). On the whole, *Characters of Worldly Young Men* presents a doubtful case for Filial Piety.

But though Kiseki was an uncertain moralist, he knew what his readers liked. Having begun with a group of unworthy sons, he went on to the obvious and entertaining subject of unworthy daughters. In 1717 he published his second character-book, a companion-piece entitled *Characters of Worldly Young Women*.[26] Its parallel title held the promise that here, too, readers would find amusing pictures of the *ukiyo*. And Kiseki is quick to assure them that modern girls are no more strait-laced than their brothers. Most of the Characters (of which there are sixteen, in six parts) confirm the view that feminine virtue is at a low ebb. Typically vain, restless, avid of new things, these alarming creatures worry their doting parents, or harass and deceive their weak husbands. The men who marry them are likely to come off very badly indeed. A 'Wayward Wife' adopts masculine dress and hair style to join parties at the Shimabara and Gion; one young woman shouts at her husband like an angry samurai; another, who deceives her parents as well as her husband to get money for her actor-lover, is at last disowned ('Even then instead of giving up love she went into business with it!'),[27] and goes off happily with the actor.

Kiseki's later character-books offer similar collections of figures of the *ukiyo*. The best of these, much admired for its mellifluous style, is *Characters of Old Men of the Floating World*[28] (1720). It too is a companion-piece to his *Worldly Young Men*, linked, moreover, by the observation that 'life flows on—sons listening to advice become old men giving it, and that within a moment'.[29] Though not so fanciful as the earlier character-books, it shows the same interest in disgraceful conduct: one gluttonous, boastful old fellow, proud of his strength, makes a series of crashing *faux pas* at his son's wedding reception; another troublesome old man wants to pledge 'brotherhood' with a boy young enough to be his grandson; still another, a rich thread merchant who 'let his own threads get tangled',[30] distinguishes himself by prolonged lechery.

With only a few exceptions, Kiseki's Characters—whet mischievous apprentices or lascivious grandfathers, spoiled daughters or their shameless, flamboyant mothers—expose weak, foolish, or wicked conduct. All the usual types of satire are represented: misers, flatterers, drunkards, boors, braggarts, gluttons, lechers. Now and then he allows his fancy to carry him to remarkable lengths (an unweaned girl bringing her nurse along to the bridal chamber), but he often deals with nothing more startling than a mild addiction, or a bit of *naïveté*. To Kiseki, a satiric realist whose humour is without bitterness, even a minor aberration, a harmless frailty or foible, may be suitable for a Character. And all the complex life of the city lay before him.

In seeking variant types Kiseki widened his explorations of *ukiyo* life and brought new subjects within the scope of fiction. Of course type-characterization was nothing new. It had already reached a medieval perfection in Muromachi popular literature: the stories called *otogi-zōshi* ('nursery tales') were peopled with stock humorous or romantic figures; the *kyōgen* farces interposed between *nō* plays, which they often burlesqued, were put together with a handful of stereotyped characters—a hen-pecked man and his shrewish wife, a stupid lord and his crafty servant, and the like. Characterizations of this lineage, but increasingly diverse, appeared in the *kana-zōshi*, and in *kabuki* and *jōruri* as well. Indeed, one of the strongest conventions of the Genroku drama was its sharply defined typology of roles: even Chikamatsu clothed his dramatis personae in the standard qualities ascribed to men and women of their social status. But Kiseki, much as he loved the theatre, preferred Saikaku's concrete, particularized descriptions of the floating world to Chikamatsu's lyrical, generalized studies of its emotional conflicts. After the manner of Saikaku, he caught the flavour of the *ukiyo* in brief, rather haphazard sketches, vivified by a sprinkling of realistic detail. And this, the random technique of his earlier fiction, served also for his Characters. Though meant to illustrate typical behaviour, they were not consistent analyses of vice and virtue.

Kiseki had too much of the unreflective Genroku spirit to care to follow abstract turns of thought. His Characters, accordingly, lack the precise focus of the pure Theophrastan genre: they do not satisfy 'the classical requirement of a well-defined moral or psychological propensity governing a number of tabulated actions'.[31] Instead, they are shaped by satirical and descriptive tendencies, such as caused the seventeenth-century English Character (despite the influence of Theophrastus) to drift from the typical towards the individual, from the universal ruling passions of men towards their curious particular eccentricities. But Kiseki was not a portrait-painter: his forte was the intimate scene, of the kind familiar in *ukiyo-e*. In his sketches of the floating world, he preferred to group his rakes, actors, courtesans, and ordinary townsmen in casual tableaux of the sort one finds in the picture-books of Moronobu and Sukenobu.

Kiseki's character-books set a fashion which other writers found it worth while to adopt. Most of his successors at the Hachimonji-ya repeated the formula mechanically: only Tada Nanrei (1698–1750), who added 'worldly mothers'[32] to the list of subjects, gave it a personal stamp. During most of the eighteenth century new character-books appeared frequently, and were popular, but their literary quality deteriorated in the course of the inevitable search for novelty. Maidservants, courtesans, mothers-in-law—even go-betweens joined the motley and at last monotonous parade.

Meanwhile the Hachimonji-ya itself had illustrated one of Kiseki's themes: the decay of worldly fortunes. In 1745, having survived his partner nearly a decade, Jishō died. His heirs struggled to carry on the business, but were slowly forced to yield to a decline which had begun before Kiseki's death. In 1767, these efforts having failed, the Hachimonji-ya printing blocks were sold to an Osaka publisher. By that time, with the *ukiyo-zōshi* near exhaustion, Kyoto and Osaka were no longer the chief literary centres. Edo, the actual seat of government, had become a city of wealth and culture, the metropolis of Japan.

But if Edo now claimed the most noted authors, and produced more books than it brought in from Kyoto and Osaka, still its new genres betrayed the powerful influence of their fiction. Hachimonji-ya adaptations from the drama, together with translated Chinese novels, provided the basic elements of the romantic fiction that later Edo writers produced in immense quantity. The satirical strain of the *ukiyo-zōshi* was continued in the 'yellow-covers' (*kibyōshi*); in sophisticated dialogue-sketches of the Yoshiwara, as well as the more dramatic stories that evolved from them in the early nineteenth century; and in the 'humorous books' (*kokkeibon*), which were simply rambling, witty excursions through the bath-houses, tea-shops, and amusement quarters of the day.

Most of the Edo writers admired Kiseki. His *ukiyo-zōshi*, especially his character-books, were widely read throughout the late Tokugawa and early Meiji periods. Even Tsubouchi Shōyō (1859–1935), the theoretician of a new Western-style realism, acknowledged their influence on his own early sketches of university life: *Characters of Modern Students* [33] (1885–86).

But the best of the later character-books had appeared in 1766: a set of modern mistresses [34] by Ueda Akinari (1734–1809), a scholarly author more famous for his polished stories of the supernatural. It seems fitting that the preface to this, the last important character-book, should contain a tribute to Kiseki and the Hachimonji-ya—and to Saikaku:

Many are the Hachimonji-ya books in which Kiseki and Jishō display our world exactly as it is. Clinging to a stout cable twisted from the strings first played by Saikaku, they draw forth the grasping spirit of the merchant. You can see the miserliness of the old man. And there are the endless caprices of the son who exhausts his patrimony in useless things: intoxicated by evil pleasures, he loses home and fortune. When you read about him, and the faithful clerk whose warnings go unheeded, and the indulgences of his mother, you cannot help thinking 'How very true!' [35]

UKIYO-E AND GENROKU FICTION

For the modern reader, Saikaku and Kiseki make rather eccentric—at times exasperating—guides to the floating world. Their language is often obscure; their minds wander erratically from one point to another; they indulge in literary allusions, private references, and jokes which are not always in the best of taste. And they take far too much for granted: the reader is addressed, flatteringly, one supposes, as an habitué of the theatre and the pleasure quarter. He is expected to be familiar with their manners and customs, their famous sights, their long-vanished actors, rakes, and courtesans.

Fortunately, scenes of the Genroku floating world were also recorded in the contemporary *ukiyo-e*. Here, in the delightfully vigorous black-and-white or hand-coloured woodcuts of the seventeenth and early eighteenth centuries, the so-called Primitives, we find sharp visual images of the people and places, the odd customs and forgotten fashions, whose strange names spangle Genroku fiction. For there is a remarkably close relationship between *ukiyo-zōshi* and *ukiyo-e*: each offers the best possible introduction to the other. Not only do they share the same social and cultural background, and the same worldly attitudes, but they share the pages of the block-printed book. Even a well-known author cannot dispense with the services of the illustrator. A Genroku book without illustrations, in some profusion, would seem as bare as a modern travel talk on the night the projector failed.

Of course there was already a long tradition of scroll-painting in alliance with literature, which had produced such masterpieces as the *Genji* scrolls. To the Japanese, the union of painting, calligraphy, and literature seemed indissoluble. One need not study the various transitional works, the specimens of early block-printing or the hand-painted manuscript scrolls of late Muromachi, to understand why Tokugawa books, beginning with a poetic anthology of 1605 and the 1608 edition of *The Tales of Ise*, included illustrations as a matter of course. Naturally these first illustrations were merely printed copies of pictures in traditional painting styles. The *ukiyo-e* style itself may be said to have begun as a result of the surreptitious interest of Tosa, and particularly Kanō painters—and their patrons—in genre subjects. *Ukiyo-e* painting has its own history, in which the woodblock prints figure as a derivative popular art. But it was this art, the specialty of a rampant trade, that offered a wider panorama of the floating world.

And the literary relations of *ukiyo-e* prints had a decisive influence on their development. Indeed, the essential character of the *ukiyo-e* style, with its warmth and intimacy in treating scenes from contemporary city life, emerged only when the anonymous middle-seventeenth-century illustrators—following *kana-zōshi* texts in which the new literary realism was also emerging—began to present their still fairly unsophisticated views of the floating world.[1] Later, after the example of Moronobu, *ukiyo-e* woodcuts were published in folding albums, or in picture-books—the usual flexible booklets of thin rice-paper stitched in double sheets. They were even emancipated to the status of single-sheet prints, distributed to publicize public beauties and actors, or sold as a substitute for the paintings which only the upper classes (and the more prosperous townsmen) could afford to buy. Yet the link remained, long after the leading *ukiyo-e* artists began to exceed all but a very few authors in popularity. Most of the great print designers were also book illustrators.

Hishikawa Moronobu (d. 1694) is commonly given credit for making the woodblock print an important art form, as Saikaku is said to have created the new school of artistic popular fiction. Both statements are over-simplified, yet it would be impossible to think of the two genres without thinking of these two men. And each recalls the other. Saikaku's characters inhabit the lively world of Moronobu's prints; Moronobu's figures—delineated with a strong simplicity of line and composition—seem quite at home in the pages of the *ukiyo-zōshi*, for which he occasionally provided illustrations. The set he did for the pirated Edo edition of Saikaku's first novel, which Saikaku himself had illustrated, shows his virtuoso ability to strike exactly the right key in transposing witty but amateurish drawings into finished, handsome designs. One wishes that there had been more such piracies, or that Moronobu and Saikaku had worked together. Indeed, their careers were roughly parallel: both men were active in the second half of the seventeenth century; both made revolutionary progress in the backward arts of the *ukiyo*. But perhaps history has been kinder to Saikaku. The *ukiyo-zōshi* writers who followed him were not so gifted, and Tokugawa fiction began its long decline before the full colour print had yet appeared. Moronobu, the first *ukiyo-e* master, has sometimes been neglected in favour of his great successors. Still it seems fair to say that he did as much as Saikaku to bridge the gap—in Japan a chasm—between popular and aristocratic art.

During his apprenticeship Moronobu acquired the techniques of the aristocratic painter. After growing up in a small provincial town, where he learned his father's trade of embroidery and textile designing, he came to Edo, the seat of the Tokugawa government, and began his years of studying the classical styles of painting. These were mainly of the Chinese-derived Kanō school, sponsored by the Shogunate, and of the native Tosa line, which had been patronized by the Court since the Muromachi Period, and had been degenerating, very slowly, almost as long. But Moronobu refused to limit himself to reproducing familiar landscapes and courtly scenes, or to painting birds, flowers, and contemplative figures in the cool mandarin vein, or even to following orthodox rules for treating the few genre subjects that had been taken up by the academicians. Still, this formal training was essential to his work: like Saikaku, he used traditional techniques to raise the level of popular art—and to enhance its popularity. Earning his living as a print-maker and illustrator, rather than a painter, he brought finesse to what was already a thriving trade.

Since most earlier block-print illustrations had been more or less inferior, the work of anonymous craftsmen, those of Moronobu opened a new era for the illustrated book. His few remaining single-sheet *ukiyo-e* are superb, the first masterpieces of their kind, but nearly all his prints were designed for publication in books or albums. Besides illustrating texts, he made a large number of picture-books, or *ehon*, in which the proportion of drawing to letterpress was at least reversed. They include picture-guides to Edo and elsewhere, illustrated anthologies of poetry, pictorial versions of *The Tales of Ise* and later classics, collections of battle-pieces, designs for fans and screens and gardens, striking erotica of all kinds, together with many other books full of the spirited people of the *ukiyo*.[2] His *One Hundred Women of Japan* and *Pictures of Japanese Occupations* have already been mentioned. In these and other picture-books, in book illustrations, in such albums as *Flower-viewing at Ueno*[3] and *Views of the Yoshiwara*,[4] Moronobu brilliantly evokes the life of the Edo floating world—and transforms it into designs that express at once its vitality and its sense of style.

Moronobu dominated his age, establishing the first great school of *ukiyo-e* artists. It is tempting to identify him with an entire 'Genroku manner'. Indeed, most of Sugimura Jihei's work used to be confidently attributed to Moronobu—until someone noticed Jihei's signature in his textile patterns.[5] Certainly many print-makers imitated Moronobu as best they could. Yet there had been at least three distinctive styles in the *kana-zōshi* illustrations of the era of creeping realism;[6] and in Genroku *ukiyo-e*, too, there were other interesting, clearly individual styles. Saikaku, for instance, was a quite eccentric illustrator: the amusing postures and queer distortions of his figures suggest the elliptical wit of his prose.[7] Moreover, his later *ukiyo-zōshi* show the characteristics of other accomplished styles. About half of Saikaku's books were illustrated by Yoshida Hambei (*fl. c.* 1665–88), whose fame in Kyoto and Osaka rivalled that of Moronobu in Edo. Among Hambei's finest illustrations are those for *The Woman Who Spent Her Life in Love*. And the quiet elegance of his manner, with its lucid composition and smooth, unaccented line, is enhanced by improved techniques of engraving and printing.

In late Genroku, as *ukiyo-e* print-making continued to flourish, technical advances were accompanied by further refinement of expression. Nishikawa Sukenobu (1671–1751) created a graceful, subtle style which was imitated as assiduously as Moronobu's. Like Moronobu, he had begun by studying the Kanō and Tosa styles, and gone on to become an *ukiyo-e* painter. But though Sukenobu was perhaps the leading painter of his time, he was also a prolific illustrator; a magnificent colourist, still he devoted a great deal of effort to designing black-and-white woodcuts. Almost all of them were book illustrations, of uniformly high quality, or print sequences to be issued in picture-books, which Kyoto people seemed to prefer to single-sheet prints. This phase of his career had of course begun when he went to work for the Hachimonji-ya, at about the same time as Ejima Kiseki.[8] After that, most Hachimonji-ya books were illustrated by Sukenobu, or by his pupils. During his long career Sukenobu produced more than a hundred picture-books, including such lavish ones as *Studies of One Hundred Women*, which the Hachimonji-ya published in 1723. So lovely were the women in these books, and in his paintings, that *ukiyo* beauties of the day were pleased to be called 'Nishikawa-style'. But he neglected none of the attractive aspects of the floating world, nor did he omit its profitable erotic side. In 1722, for instance, one of his Hachimonji-ya picture-books appeared under a title which, by a combination of puns, could mean either *Steeped in the Indigo River* or, more appropriately, *Sex at the First Encounter!* [9] There were many more of this sort.

For it was not only the robust art of Moronobu and his school that went into *shunga*, the erotic 'spring pictures'. Sukenobu's *shunga*, some of which are among his masterpieces, show his delicacy of treatment in scenes of extravagant sexual activity. Indeed, Sukenobu's erotica were so sensational that in 1722 the Bakufu issued a special, unprecedented personal ban against them.[10] Of course many equally shocking works published after that date are unmistakably his. Uninhibited sexuality, in *ukiyo* art and literature as well as in the Yoshiwara or Shimabara, was one of the few freedoms claimed by Genroku townsmen under their severely repressive system. In a thriving commercial society which made salons of its exclusive brothels and great ladies of its high-priced prostitutes, the artist was naturally interested in exploring the preoccupations of the pleasure quarter. And he was interested in making money.

Most *ukiyo-e* print-makers combined these interests, without harm to their aesthetic aims. Among the 'Primitives', the forceful theatrical artist Torii Kiyonobu and the versatile Okumura Masanobu, Sukenobu's Edo contemporary, made beautiful woodcuts of both the proper and the improper sorts.

So did Harunobu, whose sensitive, charming prints everywhere reveal the influence of Sukenobu; so, too, Kiyonaga, Utamaro, and Hokusai, to name only the greatest masters of the colour print. All these men were book illustrators as well; for the alliance between *ukiyo* art and literature remained intact long after the Genroku Era. Hokusai, in the early nineteenth century, not only illustrated an impressive number of books, most of them novels, but also wrote poetry and novels of his own. He is counted as the last of the 'three great illustrators'—the first two being Moronobu and Sukenobu.

In general, Tokugawa book illustration became more and more 'literary', as artists tried to out-rival authors by telling a complete visual story of their own. On the one hand, there was a trend towards increasingly minute realism, often executed with great skill; on the other, an obvious attempt to crowd the text into a subordinate position. Thus, in the late eighteenth-century 'yellow-covers', which continue the worldly *ukiyo-zōshi* strain, the written story is merely allowed to fill empty spaces in the pictures. But even illustrators of the long, fantastic, Chinese-style novels of that period seem anxious to provide enough detail to match the entangled plots. The contrast with the decorative effects of seventeenth-century illustrators suggests that, in the midst of technical progress, there has been some decay.

One finds a similar, if less striking, difference between early and late *ukiyo-zōshi* illustrations. Those of Sukenobu for Kiseki's *Characters of Worldly Young Men* are designed for a book of brief caricatural tales, yet have a stronger narrative quality than Yoshida Hambei's, a generation earlier, for Saikaku's novel *The Woman Who Spent Her Life in Love*. In effect, Sukenobu offers a more acceptable substitute for the stories themselves. He adds snatches of dialogue, to further the pictorial plot and characterization; he fills in more background detail, so that his pictures, if still far from Western notions of realism, convey a more intimate genre feeling. And his figures, set against these backgrounds, strike graceful but more realistic poses, show more expression, and resemble their fictional prototypes more closely. Hambei uses fewer and larger figures, arranging them in stylized compositions against uncluttered backgrounds. He shows fewer aspects of each episode: most of his illustrations present only a single scene, spread comfortably across two pages. But the crowded illustrations of Kiseki's book are usually cut into two scenes (sometimes into three or more) by walls, screens, and scalloped cloud-edges. Not that this was a new device—only, earlier book illustrators had not felt the need to make such consistent use of it.

In fact, the conventions of the narrative picture were inherited by Tokugawa illustrators from the painters of horizontal scrolls. *Ukiyo-zōshi* illustrations, too, must be scanned from right to left, as the text is printed, rather than examined from a fixed point of view. When a picture shows the same figure twice, in the adjacent rooms of a house, or on the opposite sides of a wall or screen, it is not really illogical or anachronistic, but rather designed to follow a traditional narrative principle. Thus, Kiseki's tale of the young man who wanted to be a samurai is summed up in its double-page illustration.[11] We find two groups—one in a bare-floored room and the other in an adjoining courtyard—with the same young man at the centre of each. He appears before and after his disinheritance: on the right, fencing with two shop-boys, his swords and armour displayed in the alcove and a straw archery target close at hand; on the left, subduing a fierce horse over the sprawled bodies of two attendants, before an astounded samurai. In the meantime some three years have elapsed.

Many other narrative devices may be found in *ukiyo-zōshi* illustrations. As in the scroll paintings, we see formal layers of haze floating between separate scenes. There is the psychological use of disproportion, particularly to focus attention on human figures. Houses are roofless for interior scenes, and their lines slant back defining the shallow stage according to the principles of diagonal projection. We seem to look down obliquely at these narrow, unfolding scenes, as the viewer of the horizontal scroll looks at the unwinding panorama of a more remote world. Everywhere spatial relationships are manipulated so as to embody, within handsome visual patterns, the elements of time and literary emphasis.

In this way the illustrator tells his own version of the story. He must have been expected to do more than enhance it; for the Genroku writer seems to depend on him to help create atmosphere and fill in detail. Of course, contemporary readers of a certain sophistication, even those who knew the gay quarters at second hand, through books and prints and the theatre, could supply their own visual imagery at the slightest mention of a coiffure style, a new kimono pattern, or a fashionable Shimabara tea-house. But some were not so sophisticated. For them, the word Shimabara (or Yoshiwara) itself had only a festive glow, with few real associations. And for later readers, to whom these manners and places are altogether strange, the illustrations seem indispensable.

Sometimes the artist may choose to amplify a theme which the author has succinctly stated. In Kiseki's Character of 'A Wayward Wife', for example, city matrons are said to be unduly fond of going to wrestling matches. ' "There's wrestling at Makuzu-ga-hara, and Shichigorō takes on the Thunderbolt!" they cry. "We can't miss it!" Off they dash, in sedan chairs decorated by autumn landscapes of sprinkled gold.' And the right-hand page of the illustration [12] shows one of these ladies standing near the entrance to the wrestling arena, where a sedan chair has just arrived. Another smart young woman hurries to the ticket office, past still others resting coquettishly on open-air benches along the way. Nearly half of the illustration has thus been devoted to one brief comment of Kiseki's. Again, in the middle foreground, the wayward wife sets off on one of her outrageous excursions in masculine dress—to the astonishment of a pair of fellows not mentioned in the text. On the left, she appears at a Gion party which suddenly begins to deteriorate. Here, at last, the illustrator has chosen an important scene at its decisive moment.

But the *ukiyo-zōshi* illustrator often supplies an essential part of the setting. In the letter-writing episode of *The Woman Who Spent Her Life in Love*, for instance, Saikaku describes the amorous adventure that befalls his heroine even during this interlude of respectability—and leaves it to his illustrator to create the contrasting background. Only in the picture do we see the quiet façade of her little house, its half-timbers and latticed window suggestive of a secluded Kyoto side street; within, there are the possessions—low tables, writing materials, a *koto* leaning against a Kōrinesque screen—of a refined lady who teaches etiquette and calligraphy.[13] Against this subdued background the incongruity of the heroine's behaviour becomes apparent. And the effect is heightened by adding a little doorway scene, which is Hambei's invention. The three young girls leaving on the right, under the sign 'Instruction in Calligraphy for Ladies', have had their lesson abruptly ended. Curiosity seems to have overcome a rigid training in the proprieties, at least for the girl carrying a writing-case and copybook. We see her lingering to peer through the door-curtains, as a companion turns to call her. Her line of vision points to the maid (bringing tea for the sudden visitor), to the heroine (just finishing the first line of a letter), and to the unfortunate young man himself—so out of place in these surroundings. It is perhaps the decisive moment, described in a very few words by Saikaku, in which the heroine decides to speak for herself. Throughout the book a succession of *ukiyo-e* illustrations serves to round out the scenes which Saikaku, who would agree that brevity is the soul of wit, prefers to drop before he has fully developed them. Selective as it is, the *ukiyo-e* style complements the scattered descriptive prose technique of the *ukiyo-zōshi*.

Indeed, the very difference between graphic and verbal techniques helps to explain why, in the Genroku view, they have such an affinity. Together, each with its special ability to express the static or the dynamic, the beautiful or the characteristic, they illuminate the *ukiyo* scene more brilliantly than either could alone. And the artist was accustomed to look for sources in literature—classic or contemporary. He merely treated them in his own way, to suit the Japanese taste for variations on standard themes.

Originality of treatment was what the artist sought. Thus, Moronobu did two new versions of Saikaku's own illustrations for *The Man Who Spent His Life in Love*. There is first his set for the pirated Edo edition of 1684. Although Moronobu follows Saikaku's designs, he skilfully adapts them to his own style. His new designs stand somewhere between the witty, amateurish, closely text-bound manner of Saikaku and the more decorative, freer manner of most professional illustrators. That the earlier illustrations were followed so closely suggests more than the sheer convenience of the method. The pictorial tale was itself an important part of the book. Indeed, for a picture-book edition of 1686 Moronobu prepared a new series of large, carefully done double-page illustrations, in comparison with which the text, drastically cut and printed at the top of the page, occupies a minor position.[14] But these, too, are only somewhat more elaborate treatments of the scenes chosen by Saikaku.

As one might expect, Saikaku's own illustrations are admirably suited to his novel. The novel itself seems almost to demand pictorial amplification. Each of its fifty-four chapters is only a few pages long; each, as a rule, begins with a rhetorical flourish in the allusive *haikai* vein, tells an amusing anecdote, and ends in a witticism; each is interspersed with miniature genre scenes depicting the manners and customs encountered by the hero Yonosuke in his travels. Since these scenes are evoked with a strict *haikai* economy of language, they leave much to the imagination—or to the descriptive powers of the illustrator. Often the point of an anecdote is sharpened by reference to the illustration.

One such example may be cited from the episode in which Yonosuke, at eighteen, sets off for Edo to begin an apprenticeship in trade.[15] His progress is described with poetic allusions—and references to the girls he leaves behind—as he makes his way at last to Ejiri, in the province of Suruga, where he pauses to reflect on the precariousness of the floating world. But at an inn that night he hears a pair of charming voices singing a duet. Told that they belong to the beautiful sisters Wakasa and Wakamatsu, he stays on at the inn, enjoys the favour of both sisters, and finally, giving up his trip to Edo, decides to take them along with him back to Kyoto. This leads to one of the more painful incidents of his *Wanderjahre*. It is one of those sudden changes of fortune—the uncertainty of life is a major theme in Saikaku—which may plunge anyone into sickness, poverty, jail, or even such work as running a noodle shop full tilt into bankruptcy. In the course of a journey diverted by tales of the various allurements practised on earlier guests by the two girls, who are grateful to him for having saved them from a life of evil, Yonosuke finds that he is almost out of money. Even with the girls' help, there seems to be no way of struggling on to Kyoto.

But in the village of Imokawa they ran across one of Wakamatsu's former admirers. Thanks to him, they were able to patch up an old, dilapidated, thatch-roofed house, where they settled down to the trade of making flat noodles, a local specialty.

To stop passers-by, Yonosuke would sing a snatch of song about

'drawing up my horse for shelter'—'Could it be snow?' or such.[16]
Meanwhile he would stoke the fire with one hand, never letting go his
samisen.

Thus the days drifted by, and he became even poorer. In time,
both girls settled down at the foot of Mount Hanazono, cut off their
hair, and, having been abandoned by their lover, abandoned the
world—and were truly saved from evil! [17]

So the chapter ends, with the usual ironic twist. Saikaku's
illustration shows the full extent of Yonosuke's plight: he is hard
at work in a shop for which he is indebted to Wakamatsu.
Strumming vigorously on the *samisen* to accompany his songs,
Yonosuke hunches over a flaming noodle-stove, the pile of
faggots conveniently near his right hand. Meanwhile, the two
women whom he finds himself supporting wait at the side, as a
man on horseback proceeds stolidly by. Even the gnomish
little figure leading the horse, a typical Saikaku bit of gro-
tesquerie, keeps his nose high and his gaze fixed dead ahead.
Moronobu's samurai, passing in the opposite direction, makes a
less striking emblem of bad business—just as Yonosuke, in this
version, seems less intent on his work. Substituting a tray of
bowls for the faggots is another evidence of Moronobu's
slighter concern for the anecdotal implications of the text.
Another, perhaps, is that he only hints at the shop-sign spelled
out by Saikaku (*Imokawa noodles!*), though he does add the
suggestive 'Wakamatsu-ya' shop-name on the curtain. But
Moronobu's composition and details of setting are more carefully organized, his figures handsomely grouped as well as
suavely and solidly drawn. As usual, the figures are enlarged
to bring the scene into nearer focus and enhance its pictorial
effect. Putting the traveller in black provides one of those
strong accents with which Moronobu likes to invigorate his
designs. Yet, for all the vigour of his draftsmanship, he does not
hesitate to give his designs poise and balance at the expense of
Saikaku's unstable comic exaggeration. The disproportion between the size of the passing samurai and that of the principal
figures merely follows the usual requirements of dramatic
emphasis in Japanese art—not Saikaku's extreme of shrinking
a horse to such small dimensions! [18] A horse was needed for the
scene, however, in order to point up the textual allusion to the
poem about 'drawing up my horse for shelter'. Indeed, the

VI. Saikaku and Moronobu: *The Man Who Spent His Life in Love*

Two portraits of Yonosuke at a low point in his career: accompanying himself on the *samisen* as he tries to draw customers to his noodle shop. Saikaku's

original illustration is on the left; Moronobu's two-year-later one, on the right.

contrast between the poet's lonely nobleman and the illustrator's prosaic merchant is precisely of the sort which often, within the text, is made by Saikaku's parodic turns on phrases and verses from classical literature. Instances of graphic parody of a literary theme are, of course, found throughout *ukiyo-e*. The love of an allusive linking together of disparate worlds—often to humorous effect—is not bounded by the limitations of a single artistic medium.

To be sure, Saikaku's brilliant literary gifts could hardly fail to influence his pictorial expression. Viewed from a literary standpoint, Moronobu's illustrations are more beautiful but less interesting. Moronobu is at his best in his fine double-page illustrations for the picture-book edition of *The Man Who Spent His Life in Love*, in which the text has shrunk to a thin border of excerpts along the top. The one for the third chapter shows Yonosuke at the age of nine. He is occupied in what has been cited as 'an early Japanese use of a European invention': [19] observing by telescope a large naked woman in her wooden bath-tub. It is the moment when, having suddenly noticed him, she makes a gesture of modesty—in vain. But Moronobu has given the picture an air of elegant repose. The composition is nicely balanced on its diagonal axes: on one side we see Yonosuke peering over a diminutive rooftop; below, on the other, we find the woman and her discarded kimono, with its bold design of cloud patterns and assorted crests. The suave calligraphic curves of the two figures and their garments, and the glossy blacks of their elaborate coiffures, are contrasted with neat architectural lines and abstract foliage motifs. On a subject which invites superficial realism, Moronobu has composed a pleasing and highly stylized picture.

Although Saikaku's own illustration is not so decorative, it is still further from realistic accuracy. A single page, with a drooping willow at the left, shows Yonosuke perched on a less complex but much higher roof. As he leans over at an alarming angle, he trains a long, black, sinister-looking telescope on a bulbous woman, far below, who has even odder proportions than the one drawn by Moronobu. Saikaku's picture, if less attractive than Moronobu's, is wittier, more capricious, closer to the anecdotal extravagance of this episode in the life of an *enfant terrible*. In both illustrations, however, as in the text, there is perhaps a disrespectful allusion to a scene in the third chapter of *The Tale of Genji*. Yonosuke's shameless but enterprising use of an up-to-date Western gadget recalls the more discreet spying of the young Prince Genji, between screens and sliding doors, when he glimpses a pair of charming ladies in dishabille ('This peep at everyday life was a most exciting novelty').[20] Instead of bathing, they are playing the aristocratic game of *go*.

Saikaku's literary burlesque expresses an attitude shared by the contemporary *ukiyo-e* artist. In *Genji* subjects alone—and there were many others drawn from classical literature—the prints offer an immense variety of playful treatment. Often the allusions might seem too unobtrusive, or too far-fetched, for the ordinary townsman. Yet they must have been widely appreciated, since artists went to such pains to give their work this added piquancy. For instance, Masanobu did a set of *Ukiyo-e Genji* albums (*c.* 1710), in which the noblemen and ladies of the Heian Court have become rakes and beauties of the Genroku pleasure quarter.[21] In the scene corresponding to Yonosuke's roof-top escapade a splendidly dressed young man has brazenly walked up unannounced behind a pair of courtesans, in voluminous kimono, who are playing *sugoroku*—a kind of backgammon. The scene has been transformed from a *voyeur* incident into a simple breach of etiquette. But often the taste for parody is indulged more indiscreetly: Sukenobu and Harunobu, among others, went so far as to redesign their most demure prints into startling *shunga*.

Burlesque, then, is another facet of the anomalous realism of Genroku art and literature. *Ukiyo-e* and *ukiyo-zōshi* realism have much else in common. *Ukiyo-e* illustrations suggest the generalized, genre-painting tendency of contemporary fiction, along with its anecdotal structure and spirit of comic realism, so remote from the robust picaresque tradition of early realistic fiction in the West. The slight, subtle expressiveness of *ukiyo-e* drawing, too, explains something of the relative literary disregard for characterization. These and other obvious conventions of the *ukiyo-e* style may help to modify Western notions of the importance of illusionism—or what is commonly and loosely designated as 'life'—in the realistic novel. Realism need not culminate in the sort of *trompe-l'oeil* verisimilitude that the

VII. Moronobu: Picture-book edition of *The Man Who Spent His Life in Love*

At the top is a somewhat abridged extract from Saikaku, which ends: 'Suddenly she noticed him. Speechless with embarrassment, she clasped her hands imploringly. But he only leered all the more, pointed at her, and

laughed. All she could do was jump up and scramble away barefoot, as his voice pursued her through the thin fence. "When things are quiet tonight open this back-gate and listen to what I have to say to you!" "Certainly not!" she answered—but she did it.'

skilful painter or, by tricks of his own, the novelist may achieve. The conventional lack of characterization and architectonic plot construction in the *ukiyo-zōshi* is no more a sign of weakness, or of failure to grasp and portray reality, than is the corresponding lack of literal accuracy, correct lighting, and scientific perspective in the *ukiyo-e*.

Writers and artists of the floating world express their strong sense of reality through highly formal techniques—techniques that are not at all photographic. Saikaku and Kiseki, in their way, use traditional themes and techniques as freely as do the *ukiyo-e* artists. Stylization is no less evident in the patterns of the *ukiyo-zōshi* than in those of the *ukiyo-e*: in the careful selection of detail, the decorative distortion, the lighting and composition. In these arts realistic tendencies have been accommodated to a flat, ornamental manner. There is no depth, no plausible setting in space; the characters are two-dimensional, neither modelled by shading nor attended by their shadows. And we see this already in their earliest ancestors, the Heian tales and the picture-scrolls which illustrate them. In that serene world of faultless taste, where nobles and Court ladies are poised against backgrounds of ascetic luxury, there is a similar, if more delicate, balance between the decorative and the realistic, between the claims of a subtle art and a life in which art was indispensable. But the patrician figures of the Heian Court are more reserved, smaller, withdrawn to a more distant plane. The people of the floating world could not lead such sheltered lives—nor could their arts remain aloof from the stir and bustle of their society.

VI

ECCENTRICITIES OF THE
UKIYO-ZŌSHI

THE ruling idiosyncrasy of the *ukiyo* writer is a love of spontaneity. Not only are his episodes curiously offhand, capricious, and abrupt, they may appear to have been strung together at random. Most *ukiyo-zōshi* are simply collections of stories or sketches. They are like *ukiyo-e* albums in which casually unfolded scenes—perhaps as effective in a different sequence—offer revealing glimpses of the floating world. Theme and manner hold the *ukiyo-zōshi* together. Even in those we might call novels, the chapter or episode is the fundamental unit—not the book as a whole. But there are few novels, in any sense of the term. Indeed, Kiseki's character sketches are so typical of Genroku fiction that a brief analysis of them will also describe the patterns found in most *ukiyo-zōshi*.

Structurally, Kiseki's Characters vary considerably in method and proportion; but most of them, though drawn with no strong sense of design, fit the same rudimentary formal pattern. First comes a statement of the vice or folly that the author wishes to denounce. It may be a lengthy one (if Kiseki has a really promising topic, such as feminine vanity or the degeneracy of the priesthood); or it may be an epigrammatic sentence ('Ice is colder than the water it comes from, and a worldly man out-lies the courtesans he learns from: nowadays *people* deceive *foxes*!').[1] Often the moralizing (or pseudo-moralizing) introduction has no real connexion with the point of the sketch.

The body of the Character, then, is a more or less pointed sketch dramatizing a particular vice or folly, if not always the one first introduced. This section consists ordinarily of two main scenes, bridged by a short moralizing interlude. Like the introduction, the interlude may be omitted; or it may be only a single phrase ('Thus we see fools of all kinds'). The scenes themselves, even when comparatively long, have an oddly static quality, as if they were intended to explain the *ukiyo-e* drawings that accompany them. 'A Gullible Poet', for example, is illustrated by the picture of a tradesman's son who has adopted an aristocratic pose: dressed like a courtier, surrounded by books and writing materials, he shields his eyes from the disagreeable sight of the abacus and account-book which a pair of clerks are offering him, while a sycophant leaves with one of the young master's poem-cards. This little tableau is the key situation of the sketch. After establishing it, Kiseki has only to round off his Character with a quick synopsis of the hero's unhappy fate:

Soon after the death of his father, he dissipated the family fortune and had to move to a wretched back-alley tenement in Kanasugi. His (powerfully strong) paper clothes grew tattered, and he became a (high, wide) wanderer. He borrowed money everywhere, and squandered it; he went hungry, himself a morsel for the demons; his face was so wrinkled that he looked like the poet who was called Lord Monkey.[2] Unable to compose his mind, he tilled the (ore-rich) soil and carried loads of lyrical onions.[3] Thus he walked the streets, selling the products of his deep-rooted poetic instinct.[4]

Since the words here parenthesized belong to traditional poetic diction (they are 'pillow-words', fixed epithets which Kiseki uses in punning fashion),[5] they allude ironically to the art that subverted this young man's *bourgeois* morality.

Characters often end abruptly, in a sudden climax or a witticism: an old man dying from *sumō* injuries receives a parody benediction in wrestling terms; a curio-lover reduced to beggary asks only for ancient coins. Kiseki seems anxious to wind up his sketch as swiftly as possible, once he has added a graphic scene (or two) to its generalizing introduction. But he is always concise. Settings require only a few words, mostly concrete nouns or evocative place names. A Kyoto sketch begins: 'The capital! with Higashiyama for the ornamental hills of its garden, and the Kamo's pure stream for its decorative water course, swarming with the ducks and geese of the bird shops!'[6] In another phrase or two the specific scene is identified, and the narrative begun. Local colour is sparingly applied. Yet, for all his economies, Kiseki usually manages to save his descriptive writing from thinness by his choice of significant detail. He enlivens his light, external characterizations in the same way: a diligent merchant will not pause to look at a free street show, just as one of Saikaku's 'never stumbles without picking up flints for lighters'.[7] Of course these are not rounded individuals, able to exert their own influence on the events concerning them. Kiseki's figures, however sharply drawn, live only to serve the needs of the *raconteur*. They inhabit the elusive, two-dimensional world of the anecdote—the anecdote extended, dramatized, and given a satirical edge.

Kiseki uses this sort of pattern over and over again. For example, 'A Pious Humbug' is introduced by a mildly anti-clerical sermon:

In former times clever boys, selected from childhood, were sent into the clergy, with the result that distinguished priests appeared and divine favours were granted to mankind. Nowadays, however, the matter is conducted without regard for intelligence or wit. In samurai families, those who are poor at archery and riding, or ill, so that it is difficult for them to fill government office, are persuaded to don priestly robes. Among shopkeepers, those who cannot remember the marks on a steelyard (to say nothing of calculation), and who cannot even make entries in the day-book, have their heads shaved and are initiated into the priesthood. This, on the decision of their relatives that, being unthinkable as tradesmen, they should pass their lives comfortably as priests. And so, not to mention the question of helping mankind, they even feel uneasy about their own personal affairs. Indeed, their position is one of wearing clerical dress and making a show of abstinence merely in order to demonstrate that they have become priests.[8]

And the narrative begins: 'Now there was a man who suffered a series of reverses in his youth . . .'. But he makes his fortune in the *sake* trade, only to fear that his elder son—an inordinately pious young man who cares neither for haggling at the scales nor for drinking *sake*—will lose it. So he decides to buy the boy a priesthood at a temple not far away (where he can live at leisure), and to let Jūgorō, the second son, take over the family business. The wife is persuaded; the elder son is promptly given the tonsure, settled at the temple, and made next in line to the

VIII. Sukenobu: *Characters of Worldly Young Men*

Right ('A Gullible Poet'): The elegant young man in a formal Court hat is saying, 'I can't stand the sight of an account-book!' Behind him hangs the portrait of a classical poet (and nobleman); to the right a gay-quarter crony hurries off with a poem of his about the moon. The flattered author has

been persuaded to send it to Kyoto—at some expense—in the hope that it may be included in a Court anthology. Left ('A Pious Humbug'): The priests are intent on cards, food, and *sake*: 'M-m-m, delicious!' Meanwhile, two men watch at a sliding door ('It's positively disgusting!'), and one with a lantern calls in vain at the gate.

abbot. Apparently he enjoys the life. While others are busy rattling abacuses and exchanging money, 'he takes pruning shears and calmly sets about trimming the courtyard junipers into the shapes of dragons'.

There follows a terse passage, phrased with classical suavity: 'And so the stream of time flowed by: cicadas sang on twigs from which the blossoms had fallen, snow buried the withered shoots of *hagi*,[9] and year after year came quickly to an end.' At this point Jūgorō—who has turned out to be rather wild—is sent into the custody of his elder brother. But that night Jūgorō happens to get up, and, hearing voices, peeps into the reception hall, where he sees a party in full swing. This culminating scene—of course it is illustrated—shows all the priests, his brother among them, heatedly gambling with cards and dice, gorging on octopus-meat and fish-paste, and draining bowls of *sake*. They argue and complain bitterly when one of their parishioners comes to ask them to recite Sutras over a corpse. Jūgorō reflects that his own misbehaviour is trivial, by comparison. And his father is so persuaded, too, when the temple goings-on are described to him. Instead of being disowned, the younger son is given an allowance of five hundred *ryō* a year. The sketch ends:

Having been granted this unexpected license, Jūgorō took his pleasure in any way he cared. But he had never cared for women: all his life he remained unmarried, in the grip of intense passions for one handsome boy after another. When his father died, Jūgorō handed the main house over to the clerks and, taking an allotment of a thousand *ryō* a year, moved to a separate mansion before the Chion-in gate. He bought the freedom of young actors who caught his eye, and performed plays with them, out of frolicsome exuberance. Some days he spent at *jōruri* gatherings. It was the springtime of luxury: everything to his desire, he kept a bachelor's household in which pleasures were at their height.

And this in our floating world where even priests of the Rules Sect are partial to women![10]

With his essentially anecdotal technique, Kiseki surveyed the comic possibilities of the *ukiyo*. But his anecdotes seem spontaneous, an effect augmented by traits of style. Kiseki's long, loosely co-ordinated sentences often begin and end in swift transitions: one unexpressed subject may yield to another; a single adverb may bring in a whole new scene, or indicate a major shift in time. The impression of spontaneity is left not only by careless, easy sketches, which might almost be impromptu, but by Characters of strong narrative tendency, such as the closely plotted tale of a mistaken love suicide between a young sandalwood-oil pedlar and a very deaf old woman. Sometimes Kiseki begins rather elaborately, only to drop his story as soon as he has it well under way. But eccentricity is his stock-in-trade, and he knows how to exploit it. Each Character adds another vivid portrait to the gallery of rogues, rascals, wastrels, and mere idiots.

It remained only to group Characters of a single type—unfilial sons, spoiled daughters, mistresses, or the like—into a book. So long as the character-book began and ended on a didactic note, there was no need for any over-all pattern beyond a pleasing alternation of setting and mood. And few *ukiyo-zōshi* are less haphazard. Saikaku's *Twenty Examples of Unfilial Conduct* and *The Everlasting Storehouse of Japan*, among many others, have a similarly invertebrate form; they were conceived, one supposes, as bright modern variants on the jumbled didactic books which they seem to burlesque. Even *ukiyo-zōshi* which develop a continuous narrative have a fairly ramshackle framework. The plot of *The Woman Who Spent Her Life in Love* seems scarcely stronger, as a dramatic structure, than the plan of any Genroku collection of tales. It is not so much his heroine's decline and fall that Saikaku stresses, as her erratic course from one city to another, through all the levels of society and all the careers accessible to a woman of her time. In this novel we follow once again the meandering curiosity of the classic travel diary, or rather, as in earlier confessional tales, the uncertain path of the Buddhist pilgrim's progress. But it is a new age; and tea-houses—not temples—are the chief points of interest along the way.

Sometimes the form, or formlessness, of an *ukiyo-zōshi* is meant to recall a literary prototype, since Genroku writers cultivate the incongruities of parody and burlesque. On the stylistic level, too, they seem to enjoy the incongruous mingling of elegance and vulgarity, of aristocratic and plebeian language. Seventeenth-century prose had been enriched by new elements from several sources, including that of ordinary speech; and *ukiyo-zōshi* writers were not bound by traditional canons of purity. Despite their use of the established written style, they seasoned their diction with the jargon of the pleasure quarters, the slang of Osaka shopkeepers, the sententious language of doctors, Confucianists, or anyone with a smattering of Chinese learning. A whole chorus of new voices could be heard over the narrator's monologue.

Ukiyo-zōshi writers saw nothing strange in a sudden shift from colloquial to literary language, or even to the verbal devices of poetry. Saikaku's eminence as a poet and his use of *haikai* techniques have been mentioned earlier; and Kiseki, too, whose prose is a long step nearer the plain style of modern writing, does not hesitate to admit usages characteristic of Japanese poetry.[11] One may even find an occasional 'pivot-word', so perplexing to the translator: two phrases may be linked by the double meaning of a word that ends one and begins the other. Pivot-words are not uncommon in the fanciful titles with which *ukiyo-zōshi* authors like to adorn their stories. For instance, Kiseki's *Characters of Worldly Young Women* begins with the story of an 'Influential Girl Whose Dowry Keeps Her Husband Under Her Thumb' (*Otoko o shiri ni shiki-gane no ikō musume*):[12] the pivot is *shiki*, splicing the idiom *otoko o shiri ni shiki* ('keeps her husband under her thumb'—literally, 'sits on her man') and the phrase that begins with the word *shikigane* ('dowry').

Often there is an ironic contrast between the kind of language and its subject—for example, between the high-flown poetic epithets in the last paragraph of 'A Gullible Poet' and the homely things to which they are applied. Bold spending may be described in military terms, brothel-visiting in Confucian or Buddhist ones; and such a contrast may extend throughout an entire work, as in Kiseki's *Courtesans Forbidden to Lose Temper*. Indeed, parodic techniques account for much of the flavour of Genroku writing. And there are a great many kinds of parody in Tokugawa literature. Nearly every genre was parodied—in poetry Chinese as well as native forms—and all the Heian, Kamakura, and Muromachi classics received this sort of attention. An historical account would have to discuss such antecedents as early *haikai* verse and *kyōgen* burlesques of *nō* plays.

But within Tokugawa fiction alone there are many levels of parody, ranging from near-imitation and faintly amusing pastiche to the most grotesque and indecent travesty.

Parodies of various kinds mark the progress of Tokugawa realism. In the early seventeenth-century *kana-zōshi* era one departure from literary tradition, from courtly ideals to *bourgeois* realities, was accomplished by altering *The Tales of Ise* (*Ise monogatari*) to *The Fake Tales* (*Nise monogatari*).[13] Parodying this deeply respected classic was surely as much a desecration as it was for Kiseki, later, to parody the Buddhist sermon style. And it was done by the crudest of methods: verbal alteration, the literary equivalent of adding a moustache to the *Mona Lisa*. But if the method of *The Fake Tales* seems primitive, still it was applied with scrupulous industry. The scholarly author has retouched each of the 125 episodes with a Rabelaisian sense of humour. Often he converts classic romance to modern gluttony, not overlooking the sexual symbolism of food.

The Tales of Ise was the victim of further parodies, too, although most of them could be more strictly defined as burlesques reinforced by occasional direct parody. And the other classic tales were treated in similar fashion. For example, in 1710 a Hachimonji-ya competitor, possibly Nishizawa Ippū, published *The Gay 'Tale of the Heike'*.[14] In this book the long, complex epic of the fall of the Taira Clan (Heike) has dwindled to an *ukiyo* adventure. As usual, the only warfare is the battle of the sexes: all the heroes have been transferred from the late Heian battlefield to the Genroku pleasure quarter. Taira Kiyomori has become Taira Iromori, the son of Saikaku's character Yonosuke. When the story begins, Iromori is at the zenith of his power—as a rakish, free-spending man about town. Ignoring the warnings of a faithful retainer, he continues to indulge his extravagant tastes, particularly for the expensive beauties of the Kyoto pleasure quarters. One of his changes of affection results in a mock version of the pathetic story of Giō, the dancing-girl who lost Kiyomori's favour. Iromori makes expeditions to one gay quarter after another, and also entertains luxuriously at his mansion in Rokuhara. Finally, after many campaigns, he reaches the Edo Yoshiwara. During his carousal there, a messenger from Kyoto brings the advice, from his old family retainer, that he should hurry back to observe the thirty-third anniversary of his father's departure. This he does, and one night Yonosuke appears to him in a dream and warns him to beware of sensuality. Yonosuke's harangue ends with an eloquent phrase or two about the evanescence of earthly joys. But the vision suddenly dissolves into the dawn clouds, a cock crows, a bell rings, and Iromori wonders why his servants don't hurry up with his tobacco, his basin of water, and his breakfast.

Thus the heroics end with a final lapse into the quotidian. And just as the poetic opening passage of *The Tale of the Heike* sets the melancholy tone of the entire chronicle of war, death, and vanished splendours, so a direct parody of it, at the beginning of *The Gay 'Tale of the Heike'*, establishes the mock-epic character of this story. Here are the first few lines of the thirteenth-century work:

The bell of the Gion Temple echoes the impermanence of all things. The pale flowers of the teak-tree show the truth that they who prosper must fall. Pride lasts but a little while, like a spring-night's dream.

And then their irreverent but not unpoetic eighteenth-century version:

The bells of the Gion Festival echo the impermanence of all guests. The pale faces under the cherry-tree show the truth that they who drink must stagger. Dancing lasts but a little while, like a midsummer-night's dream.[15]

Of course the Hachimonji-ya published *ukiyo-zōshi* of this sort too. Kiseki's *Courtesans Forbidden to Lose Temper* (1711) was the most popular of all Hachimonji-ya books—to the late-Victorian dismay of W. G. Aston, who wrote:

It is not a novel, but a debate on a subject of which I must renounce the attempt to give an idea. In so far as mere words go, there are more objectionable works, but the whole attitude of the author is profoundly immoral. What is specially unpardonable is his irreverent use of terms borrowed from the Buddhist religious vocabulary, and the scandalous way in which here and elsewhere the great names of Japanese history are dragged by him through the mire. Its humour, however, is undeniable.[16]

Doubtless Genroku readers were not so shocked by Kiseki's attitude as they would have been by Aston's, since their own attitude towards religion, as towards sex, was often shamelessly humorous. Yet it must be admitted that sacrilegious parody runs throughout the book. Its Japanese title *Keisei kintanki*, which has a distinctly sermonizing ring, is later expounded by an appropriate text from Master Saikaku's *Ichidai nangyō* (*The Sutra of the Man Who Spent His Life* . . .). Also, by a double pun, *kintanki* alludes at once to a well-known work of sectarian controversy (the *Kindangi*) and to the genre of the popular Buddhist sermon, or *dangi*. Both these manners are burlesqued here and there among the twenty-four otherwise typical *ukiyo-zōshi* sketches which make up the book. Besides imitating a heavy theological style, perverted by such puns as *Saihō jorō* (Shimabara prostitute) for *Saihō jōdo* (Paradise, the Western Pure Land), Kiseki does indeed make scandalous use of the great names of Japanese history. He begins, for example, by announcing that he will vindicate the ancient and orthodox Doctrine of Heterosexual Love (established by the gods Izanagi and Izanami) [17] against the heresy of that other sect which was founded by Kōbō Daishi [18] some centuries ago in a monastery near Kyoto. Evidently there is nothing sacred.

Yet Western literature, too, has had a considerable vein of Scriptural parody since at least the twelfth century. During the medieval 'outburst of monkish pleasantry', as it has been called, religious subjects held the chief place in burlesque and parody. 'The complete service of the Mass was applied to the worship of Bacchus and Venus. . . . Erotic stories were told in the language of the Bible. Saints' lives were parodied. In short there was no language too sacred for the monkish parodist to defile, no ritual too solemn.' [19] Moreover, this sort of profanation was not only tolerated but accepted as a literary convention. Certainly Genroku attitudes permitted a great deal of licence in this respect. Bakufu censorship of fiction was erratic in the extreme, but mainly watchful for overt political satire. Among readers as well as writers there seems to have been no feeling that flippancy or humour was incompatible with religious belief. Nor is the tone of this fiction always of a goliardic coarseness. Sometimes it has the delicate lyricism of one of the *ukiyo-e* prints in which, to suggest a parallel, a beautiful

courtesan may be seen posed in the iconographic setting of a
Bodhisattva. *Ukiyo* fiction, like *ukiyo* art, uses even remote
analogies and very odd transmogrifications.

To be sure, Kiseki does not care to write pure parody, or
pure burlesque. He uses these elements because they set off his
sketches of *ukiyo* high life, and because they express so well the
bright, satirical, rather cynical attitudes which were cultivated
in that world. Then, too, Saikaku, whom he admired intensely,
had used parodic techniques in his own *ukiyo-zōshi*—and for the
same reasons. Not that Saikaku, either, made any attempt to
write strict parody. Comic distortions of bits of well-known
prose and poetry are scattered throughout his works, as a
glance at a commentary will show; but, beyond that, he seems
content to imply a casual burlesque reference from his comparatively frivolous *ukiyo-zōshi* to popular or classic literature.
Some of the resemblances between *The Man Who Spent His Life
in Love* and *The Tale of Genji* have already been mentioned:
there are many others among the fifty-four chapters that make
up each of these books. Most important, though, Yonosuke is
clearly a Genroku descendant of Lady Murasaki's ideal
amorist, Prince Genji; for the chief use of this extended
literary allusion is to refer obliquely from *bourgeois* to courtly
life and love. Out of that ironic contrast comes a heightened
sense of the commercial romantic values, and prices, of *ukiyo*
society.

Much of the acid wit of Saikaku's fiction is distilled from
the sentimental atmosphere of the old-fashioned romances.
Old-fashioned exemplary tales were easily burlesqued too, as in
his *Twenty Examples of Unfilial Conduct in Japan*. Since the
Chinese *Twenty-four Examples of Filial Conduct* was quite familiar
to his readers, Saikaku's ridicule of that worthy book could
scarcely be lost on anyone. Another kind of burlesque may be
discerned in *The Woman Who Spent Her Life in Love*. Here,
using the didactic manner of Buddhist confessional fiction, but
with a liberal seasoning of wit and pornographic detail, Saikaku
wrote a dramatic confession more sensational and yet more
artistic than *Moll Flanders*. One does find much that is sordid,
related with naturalistic candour. But there is also much
sophisticated amusement, to which the parodic implications of
this outrageous confession add the same sort of irreverent

mockery that shocked Aston in Kiseki. True, Saikaku's heroine has reformed. She is living in seclusion at a vine-clad little shelter that seems to be the stage-setting for another medieval tale of withdrawal from worldly concerns. But she has withdrawn to her 'Hermitage of Voluptuousness', as she calls it, only after having seen the images of her former lovers— as many of them as could be represented—in a group of statues of the Buddha's Five Hundred Disciples. And she tells her remarkable story with relish; she never tires of explaining how irresistible she was. Her experiences have apparently left her with a cheerful worldly cynicism, very far indeed from the saintly attitude appropriate to a woman who has repented her sins and renounced the world. Sometimes the remarks with which she ends an episode (one recalls her comment on the misfortune of a lack of virility, particularly for a woman) have a racy unconventionality that seems to parody the hackneyed moralizing of the usual confessional tale. Indeed, her final words ('You may call it a trick of my old trade—but how could my heart be so impure?') remind us adroitly that pseudo-confession, pretending to open one's heart to another, was one of the wiles of the accomplished courtesan. She had used the same trick on other gentleman-guests to win their sympathy . . . and we recall that when she greeted the two young men who came to her hermitage (to learn about the ways of love) she smiled and exclaimed 'Gentleman-guests even now!'

Burlesque of this kind was one of the indulgences of Genroku fiction. And not only literary works, individually or as types, but customs, institutions, and kinds of people were frequently burlesqued. The hyperaestheticism of the tea ceremony, or of flower-viewing, the pedantic jargon of the Confucianist, the swagger of underpaid samurai—these, too, were often ridiculed. Kiseki's Characters include many such types, since, with the themes of corruption and affectation, he could safely lampoon members of the higher orders: a pious boy turns into a dissolute, hypocritical priest; a would-be poet, the son of a cotton merchant, imitates the fastidious elegance of Court nobles; an ignorant young man who quotes the Confucian *Analects* by the hour enjoys a brief career as a quack doctor. But whether burlesquing literature or life, Genroku writers were able to examine and criticize their own society at the same time that they amused it. For the incongruity thus exploited was exactly what heightened their sense of the reality of their own world. In Japan, as in the West, parody and burlesque were important techniques in the development of realism.

Perhaps it is not strange that these realistic tendencies were at last frustrated: after all, *ukiyo-zōshi* writers had no critical programme (social or artistic), nor any bias towards an objective plain style, rational motivation, or full-blown scientific description. What they did have was a vitality that derived from a fundamental change in literature, a change towards closer integration into a cultivated, thriving, commercial society. And the youthful exuberance of their manner does not diminish its charm. When Meiji writers and critics, weighed down by the imported methods of the Victorian novelists, looked back at Genroku fiction, they often sighed for what seemed a lost state of grace. They had become socially respectable, they were almost too conscious of the gravity of their work, but they longed for the retrospective pleasures of that age, and for the exhilaration of its naïve *rapprochement* between literature and society. That the floating world had sunk into history only gave its fiction the pleasure-sad tone so much esteemed by the Japanese in their literature. The tales of the *ukiyo* had acquired an appealing tinge of nostalgia.

From

Characters of Worldly Young Women

by Ejima Kiseki

CHARACTERS OF WORLDLY
YOUNG WOMEN

Kiseki begins his second character-book in customary fashion with a lively tirade. And he treats that most ancient subject of satire: feminine perversity. In the Characters to follow all its latest varieties will be illustrated. Here, then, is the long censorious passage (in part borrowed from Saikaku) with which he introduces his book of sketches of these modern hussies:[1]

IT was once believed that excessive virtue is typical of young ladies. Now, however, mother and daughter alike behave immodestly: they ape the manner of harlots and courtesans, and of the actors who play female roles; they wear their sashes so high one thinks of the pictures of Ling-chao [2] (without her fish-basket); their sleeves hang open in the masculine style; and on promenade they saunter with a seductive gait. They do everything for effect, caring only how others see them. A facial blemish is hidden by choosing the right profile; thick ankles are concealed in a long skirt; a large mouth is abruptly closed, at the cost of swallowing a remark. Ah, the women of today go to extraordinary lengths! If their husbands could bear it, these ladies would no doubt scrape and polish into their very nostrils, regardless of pain. They abhor stray hairs straggling at the back of the neck, and pluck every one of them, down to the slightest fluff. In their own tidying-up they all but heap ornamental mounds of sand.[3]

And since, as people say, inferiors learn from their betters by imitating them, it is natural that all the maids—personal attendants, parlour-maids, even kitchen-girls whose right hands bear the mark of the ladle—should whet the fish-slicer, shave their eyebrows, cut the short hairs in the hollow of the neck, put rice bran in an old tea-bag, and, after soaking for hours in a hot tub (each heedless of the others), scrub themselves furiously. Having no idea when to stop, they end with a hideous inflammation of the skin.

Few women of former times—courtesans excepted—used oil of aloes-wood, but now young ladies smear it on down to their navels. To think of keeping a wife these days you must be prepared to increase your expenses, not only by the cost of her food, but also by a round box of five *ryō* in gold, handed over the first thing every morning. 'A fair skin hides ten defects', she says, and masks herself in a thick coat of powder, even if her face would be bearable undisguised. Still the result is unfortunate. Neglecting what seems out of sight, she gives her neck and shoulders the two-toned colouring of an Anraku-an brocade.

And the reason why modern girls have become altogether *too* smart, till indeed they are as gaudy as harlots, is that their mothers, being soft-headed, pride themselves on daughters of quite mediocre looks. They dress them in striking clothes, take them along to shrines and temples where large crowds gather, and delight in having licentious men stop to stare after them. Noses high, they walk on, thinking, 'Doubtless no one else in the world has such a daughter!' And there are mothers still worse. . . .

A woman who is mistress of a large household may be known to have had five children—one a year, the eldest now thirteen. Yet for sightseeing and temple-visiting she decks herself out in gorgeous clothes, and adopts the wanton air of a courtesan. Though her wailing children run after her (crying, 'Mamma, can't we go?'), she shuts them up in the house, assumes an expression as unmatronly as possible, and sets out to display herself to fashionable men.

Thus, no matter if she happens to be chaste at heart, her inclination to love finery more than her children, and to seek out crowded places, causes her to forget home, children, and parents, and, not unnaturally, to win a spicy reputation among the young rakes.

In general, it may be said that a woman's morals nowadays are as changeable as a cat's eyes. When she returns in the evening from a picnic to look at flowers, if you notice, she appears to have lost character since morning. She has nimbly removed her cotton socks and stuffed them into her sleeves; she has thrust a wooden skewer into her hair, to replace the silver bodkin, and put the tortoise-shell comb away in her purse; she has tucked her scarlet crêpe underskirt into her sash, and lowered the (to her) unpleasantly high neck-line of her outer garment. Her silk veil has been put in the travelling-box, and the blind-stitched white satin band of her Kaga hat rolled in with a supply of towels and paper handkerchiefs, and given to a servant to carry. At dusk she gleefully hitches up her skirt like a peasant girl going to weed a rice-field, and her conduct becomes so loose that you can hardly tell Madam from kitchen-maid. Tipsy on *sake*, and chanting ballads in a shrill voice, she goes home by way of Yasaka-hakken and Nawate where she knocks on tea-house doors and peers in at the courtesans. Kyoto women cannot be equalled for boldness—certainly not by their men!

Again, leggings used to be worn only by the firewood-selling women of Yase and Ohara; but in recent years, thanks to the advance in sophistication, even ladies of prominent family have grown tired of ordinary underthings: each step (to the secret chagrin, surely, of their maids) reveals a glimpse of red silk gaiter. To protect their collars in the back, they use pale blue pongee wraps; to keep the dust from their oil-stiff, pinned coiffures, they order waterproof hats in the style worn by nobles at Court. One supposes that they dress for a solitary trip to the country as if going to hear the oracle at Kashima.[4] Lately, too, ladies wearing oiled-paper raincoats, in the fashion of maidservants from samurai households, have been seen in the capital.

With the modern urge to be fashionable, little girls of seven or eight have precocious whims. Bored with the way their hair has been done, they say, 'A "hanging Shimada",[5] please, the back hair drawn in; and tie it with one of those smart hidden cords.' And a girl going off to marry no longer drenches her sleeves in tears, weeping at the farewell. The young lady of today is cheerful enough, if a bit impatient with the go-between. She hurries to get ready, jumps into the sedan chair (which she has eagerly awaited), and radiates joy from the very tip of her nose. In particular, the girl brought up in Kyoto acquires a knowing air long before the provincial one: she becomes an expert in coquetry. Should she lack a teacher, looking around would soon teach her to look out for herself.

In a world where such manners prevail, a girl who asks,

'Mamma, where do babies come from?' and who, at sixteen or seventeen, has been so sheltered by her parents that she is unfamiliar with the paths of love, thinks of men only as terrifying creatures, blushes violently at the slightest touch, and, if anyone snatches at her sleeve or skirt, does not hesitate to scream—a girl of this sort embarrasses men, and is referred to as 'That old-fashioned simpleton!'

But should a proper young lady behave otherwise?

A WAYWARD WIFE

In this little tale, with its typically abrupt ending, Kiseki offers a Genroku variation on the traditional theme of the spoiled, restless wife. There is also her indulgent husband, 'his nose tilted as triumphantly as if he were the Emperor Hsüan Tsung'.[1] Indeed, the wife herself seems to be an analogue of Hsüan Tsung's exquisite consort Yang Kuei-fei, often portrayed in paintings (even ukiyo-e travesties) as playing the flute for the doting Emperor. This 'Wayward Wife', too, is musically inclined. Possibly the rout she causes should remind us that Yang Kuei-fei, the peerless beauty, was blamed for the An Lu-shan Rebellion!

'OBVIOUSLY morning-glories are best at morning,' declares the mistress, 'not to say how much cooler it is.' And so that night she leaves orders to fill tiers of lacquer boxes with savoury rice and a variety of titbits, prepared exactly to her taste, to arrange several chairs at a back hedge as far as possible from the house, and to lay a floral carpet. 'Cedar picks for the food, a gold lacquer tray . . . be sure to use that exquisite tea from Toga-no-o! Have the bath ready before six. As to my hair, you may do it in three folds, and please take out a sheer gown with wide sleeves and a pink lining—the sash ought to be dark grey satin, covered with huge dots, the underskirt white, but with a speckled pattern. It must all seem quite perfect: you know how the neighbours stare. So put the maids in fresh summer kimono, won't you? And do send a sedan chair to Kama-no-za for my sister, at the usual rising time.' After issuing a bewildering set of instructions to her housekeeper, who has long had charge of kitchen affairs, she retires to lie at ease in the shelter of an ample mosquito net; and tiny bells tinkle at its corners as the servants fan her, by turns, till she drops off to sleep.

Such are her airs merely to look at flowers in her own garden.

And modern matrons have their other caprices, too.[2] They reserve three boxes for the latest play, but then, stopping at Chōraku Temple to hear ballads chanted when an image is on view, become so absorbed they omit to go to the theatre. Yet their boredom is not easily dispelled by the suitable feminine pleasures of incense-guessing, poem cards, playing the *koto* or the *samisen*, painting, and flower-arranging. 'There's wrestling at Makuzu-ga-hara, and Shichigorō takes on the Thunderbolt!' they cry. 'We can't miss it!' Off they dash, in sedan chairs decorated by autumn landscapes of sprinkled gold.

Did anyone hear of women at wrestling matches in former times? But since men now dote on their wives, and meet each request with a nod, and a smile of fatuous tolerance, these ladies do not hesitate to display their morbid zest for outings—with picnic lunch—to watch the beheading of criminals at Awataguchi. It recalls how Chieh-chi, consort of King Chou of the Yin Dynasty, having exhausted her notable repertoire of diversions, found a superior pastime in seeing executions by the 'wrapping and roasting' process; or how King Yu of Chou, infatuated with Pao-ssu, had the signal-fires set off to amuse her. Indeed, these are only classic examples of the familiar petticoat tyranny. The greengrocer need simply say, 'Madam's orders', to be paid off in large coins for water-melons costing 365 *momme*; and no sooner has he gone than two stout bearers are dispatched to Yakichi's, on Shijō, to settle a 28,326 *mon* account for vegetable jelly. You may imagine the other luxuries. Smoking, for instance, used to be unknown as a feminine practice, except among courtesans; yet today women who abstain are as few as monks who fast.

Now there was a certain man who, though of merchant lineage, was highly esteemed, being known throughout the capital for his wealth. Generations ago his family had withdrawn from all but the infrequent business of handing down superb heirlooms. When snow fell he performed the tea ceremony; at blossom time he wrote poems in a traditional vein. He was careful to ignore whatever might be considered practical.[3]

As a husband, he behaved with impeccable lordliness, never glancing into the kitchen. His wife, a radiant beauty, was the irregular offspring of a person of rank. Not only was she adept in the poetics of an ancient school, she had a rare gift for music, and particularly for the reed-pipe: frost gathered in midsummer when she blew winter melodies; with longevity tunes she made her husband utterly feeble. She was addicted to the pursuit of elegance, whether in arts or manners. For summer nights she had her room screened from mosquitoes by panels of silk gauze: inside were placed a five-foot-square tray-garden and a floating lamp, as well as fireflies specially procured from Uji and Seta.[4] Thus she relieved the discomforts of hot weather. In winter she warmed herself at a covered brazier large enough for eight people, and had little girls with bobbed hair chafe the soles of her feet. Husband and wife slept in the perfume of precious incense, while its smoke, in all the varieties of Fuji, Asama, and Muro-no-yashima,[5] curled through their clothing. Devotees of the cult of fragrance, they lived in a style of unfailing splendour. Where the father had strewn the seeds of riches the son now possessed mountains wooded in silver-bearing trees. Interest money clattered incessantly in his scales—a vulgar sound, to be sure, but better than party music at a poor man's house. No one carrying an account book visited his mansion on the last day of the year: all bills were paid early in November, as if the New Year (not greeted by the customary gate-pines) had arrived too soon.

Yet his wife was unhappy. Though she lived in luxurious fashion, and though her husband was handsome and urbane, a man who, far from counting among the Twenty-four Paragons of Filial Piety, was more devoted to wife than mother—despite all this good fortune, which would seem to have left no desire unfulfilled, she perversely disliked being a woman.

One thought obsessed her: 'Why was I cursed with this sex? Tied down to a skinny devil, and no chance to enjoy myself as I please!'

Boldly she extracted her husband's consent to have her hair trimmed in masculine style, the rich pinned coiffure replaced by a boyish arrangement in two folds, with the back hair drawn up. In dress, too, she flouted convention: a short skirt (exposing an edge of lining), a coat of 'eight-roll' [6] cloth, a gold-mounted sword, medium long, and a wide rush hat of the 'Mist-on-Fuji' kind. Thus attired, and accompanied by her husband, she set out each day on another, more distant excursion. 'Let's climb Mount Kōya', she would say. 'Those monks are so terribly woman-shy they'll be fun to tease.' Or: 'Now let's go to the whale-spearing at Kumano Bay.' Her demands were endless.

Surely if men yielded to all such whims, these hussies would insist on going to China—'to see the castle of that fellow Coxinga [7] one hears so much about'.

But since the poor husband had a genius for being hood-winked, he delighted in her singular conduct ('How original to dress up like a man!'), and even took her along to the Shima-bara. When they were shown into a reception-room at Hana-bishi-ya, he said, 'See what a dashing wife I have! You won't find such a curiosity-seeker in all China; and as for looks—well, I'm afraid your famous beauties are a little outclassed. Smart, isn't she?' And he engaged the most celebrated cour-tesans, for his wife as well as himself. They gave pleasure their undivided attention: doubtless the voluptuous joys of Paradise were exceeded.

One day this couple went to a fashionable tea-house in Gion; and there, with the aid of professional jesters, [8] they held a lavish and rather noisy party. The husband began to boast of his wife's accomplishments. 'You girls should hear her play the reed-pipe', he said. 'I suppose you're on good terms with men of discrimination, and you've heard all kinds of music, but it may be that a really expert artist on this instrument has not yet performed in Gion.'

At this the proprietor and his wife bowed low, pressing their foreheads tightly to the matting. 'Never,' they assured him, 'not once in all the years since the God of Gion deigned to come here from India. But if Destiny now grants us the privilege of hearing your lady on the reed-pipe, clearly we were born at an auspicious hour.'

Elated by these words, he exclaimed, 'Come, Madam! You must outdo yourself for this audience.' And he settled com-fortably back against the pillar of the alcove, his nose tilted as triumphantly as if he were the Emperor Hsüan Tsung.

His wife, who was of course a virtuoso, chose the song that Chang Liang [9] played on Chiu-li Mountain during the battle between Han and Ch'u, the song beginning, 'When the autumn wind drives the leaves, and the traveller thinks of his far-off home . . .'. And she poured out all her skill.

In the next room, strange to say, an uproarious party lapsed into melancholy. Hitherto lively guests reflected on the evil of squandering money that had been earned by the sweat of their

IX. Sukenobu: *Characters of Worldly Young Women*: 'A Wayward
Wife'

The placard at the upper right announces: 'Grand Presentation of *Sumō*
Wrestlers From All Over'. And the woman hurrying to buy her wooden
ticket says, 'I must see the Thunderbolt!' Below, on the right, two young men
chant a current ballad of a love-suicide ('The Kawara-bashi oil-seller's . . .'
'. . . only daughter was called O-Some'), and one of the girls on the bench

exclaims 'Marvellous!' To the left, the wife goes off on a masculine sort of
excursion ('The *tayū*'s waiting!'); while beyond, in a pair of adjoining party
rooms, she plays the reed-pipe as her husband declares, 'There's no master
like my wife.' Next door an effeminate youth empties his *sake* into the hollow
cup-stand, a courtesan stops playing the *samisen*, a patron dips into his purse
as he prepares to take sudden leave. . . .

parents; they felt inclined to go home without waiting for the supper already ordered. The charming boys called in to add to the gaiety remembered their native villages, and how their true fathers had toiled under cruel burdens, barely able to get along from one day to the next. *Samisen* in hand, they sat with tears shining in their eyes. No one asked the company of the house courtesans, who for that matter (though it was time to settle monthly accounts) were reviving nostalgic memories, and feeling they had landed in a somewhat thorny bed of roses. 'The other girls have the knack of it,' remarked their mistress obliquely, 'but our kites are too tail-heavy to get off the ground.' Even this seemed to pass unheard, and their sorrowful expressions did not alter. Squirming with reluctance, they withdrew into a dark room ('Oil lamps are expensive . . .'); they wanted tea, but shrank from troubling anyone; and as they talked of their holidays, now regretted, they wept freely.

But the girls who were on their own had begun to choke and sniff a bit, too. Oblivious of the guests, they told each other their grievances. 'No matter if we work so hard we have to strip down like wrestlers, meals and clothes cost a lot, and it's a struggle to make ends meet. But how else can we earn a living?'

The jesters worried about the annual reckoning, which was not yet near, and thought, 'Better to run away from all this, or hang yourself and be done with it!' They dropped their game of capping humorous verses. 'It's a miserable life', they sighed. 'We jesters have to drink when we'd rather not; we have to praise the tiresome little songs of our patrons, hear ourselves called fools by real blockheads, force a smile if we're offended, and tell a roomful of people what even a woman would keep secret. No, there's nothing so bitter as to entertain for a living. If you happen to please, you may be hired five times and get only one *bu*, or two at most. In this wide world, is there no country where it rains hard cash?' [10] Folding their hands, they contemplated the vanity of all things.

Even the staunchly avaricious proprietor and his wife were somehow or other seized by an extraordinary fit of conscience. 'If only we could do business without lying!' A single note had scattered their wits, and they shed unexpected tears.

Just then several guests appeared at a doorway leading from

an inner room. 'I've always found it gay here,' one of them commented, 'but today is odd—you might as well be marooned on Demon Island.' He exchanged a few inappropriate household remarks with a courtesan (hired out of his own pocket), compassionately handed her an extra coin, wiped his eyes, and left the tea-house at once.

From

Characters of Worldly Young Men

by Ejima Kiseki

CHARACTERS OF WORLDLY
YOUNG MEN

*Kiseki's first and most famous character-book opens with a generalized
sketch of the inverted filial piety which is the theme of most of the Characters
to follow. With the aid of Saikaku, as ever, he begins by illustrating the
regrettable truth of a pessimistic adage:* [1]

MANY years ago it was observed that 'A father slaves, his
son idles, and the grandson begs'. This proverb, if scarcely
witty, is indeed a wise one: it seems to anticipate the behaviour
of modern children, and its truth is still keenly felt.

A man will ignore the moon and flowers, which most people
are fond of, and keep his mind fixed on the abacus. He never
varies his diet of pickled vegetables by so much as a single red-
snapper in the running season ('The idea!'); mushrooms may
be as cheap as ten for two *fun*, but he merely glances at them in
passing. To quench his thirst he drinks hot water flavoured
with parched rice. He lights a single oil lamp in the middle of
the house, and puts it out when he goes to bed—comforted, if
mice run riot, by the thought that they will find no tempting
fish in his cupboard. Summer and winter he works in a sleeve-
less undershirt, and he wears nothing finer at Bon [2] or the New
Year. He always strains for economy. Blinded by parental love,
he struggles on till he turns grey-haired, thinking, 'When I've
saved up enough money for the boy . . .'. Though he gives his
son luxuries, he himself toils like a clerk. He refuses to let his ten
thousand *kamme* [3] of silver enjoy the world, preferring to make
his storehouses groan.[4]

Thus he drives himself frantically to death. And since the
old man even hated to part with a cast-off wadded garment, as
a gift to a relative or servant, not one chopstick is lost: money,
houses, storehouses—down to the ashes under the kettle—come
by inheritance to the only son, without the slightest effort on his
part. Profits from the well-established business, or from rentals

and loans, pour in so steadily that the young gentleman decides his father was foolish to give himself useless trouble—when he could have lived comfortably without running a large establishment and straining every nerve at trade. Considering it a matter of no importance, at about twenty the son gives up business altogether. He equips himself superfluously with a bamboo cane and a round cap, and has a long-handled umbrella held over him; he displays an air of affluence, caring nothing for the opinion of others. 'I shall spend my money as I choose', he may say, but he is disregarding the will of Heaven. A man lacks understanding till thirteen, takes orders from his father till the mid-twenties, after that works on his own, and by forty-five, settled for life, reaches the age of self-indulgence.

How is it, then, for a man to say that he is 'retiring early', and to stop work in his prime? He dismisses many retainers, who, deceived in their reliance on him, are forced to seek new masters, and are exposed to hardships. While other people are busy settling their accounts for the half year, he orders his own blind *samisen*-player to perform, his wife to play the *koto*, and a maid to serve tea. In everything he takes the nonchalant attitude of a man of leisure. He shows more interest in his daily extravagances than in calculating for the future, and the money his father had saved trickles slowly away. Soon there are gaps in his finances, and even those in his roof go unmended. At last the grandson is left without so much as a place to live.

And Kiseki gives further examples of the waywardness of spoiled children. He ends by pointing out that even disowning a son does not necessarily force him to change his ways:

A boy whose conduct has been bad enough for disinheritance is rarely led to repent his past errors and reform his character. Instead, he takes the attitude that it's fun to be disowned; quite unabashed, he goes among evil companions, jesters and sedan-chair bearers. 'With your family's money,' they tell him, 'your old man's a skinflint to disown you for spending one or two thousand *ryō*. Don't give it another thought!' Thereafter he is isolated from decent people and is gradually enticed into a villainous gang. He learns the fine points of the various kinds of extortion, causes a great stir in the neighbourhood, and makes his father burn with anger. Never showing the slightest virtuous intention, he becomes a true rascal. 'Very well!' he thinks. 'Even if my father won't help me, I'll not beg.' So he panders for harlots at ten per cent, serves as procurer for the badger-game, devises swindles involving imaginary mines and re-claimed fields—and becomes a hundred times worse than ever.

A SPENDTHRIFT

This is another of Kiseki's curious extended anecdotes, another burlesque of the bourgeois scion who has developed the refined tastes of the feudal lord, or of the still precious, if sadly impoverished, member of the Court nobility. Rich and unpractical young men might cultivate the arts of poetry, flower arrangement, and the tea ceremony, along with such aristocratic sports as light archery (performed from a sitting position) and kemari, a mild ceremonial kind of football played in formal costume. Doubtless some found these pursuits so engrossing that they 'coveted Lu Yang's spear'—brandished to check the sun from setting before the end of a decisive battle. But it was seldom that their aestheticism kept them from enjoying the delights of the ukiyo. Even Kyoto, the classic city of temples, palaces, and gardens, supported a number of thriving pleasure quarters. Like the 'Wayward Wife', the 'Spendthrift' visits both Gion, on the east bank of the Kamo River, and the Shimabara. And he attends a memorable party.

A CERTAIN man was master of a house which displayed the long dark-blue curtain of the money-changer, one of those serious traders in the yellow roses and golden flowers now in full bloom. People called him 'lucky', because no one had lost a single *momme* left on deposit there; and as his trade flourished he gradually expanded his shop and bought out his neighbours. He supported a way of life far different from that of a decade before. When his wife now made a pilgrimage she wore a Kaga hat and needed a stream of serving-women to carry her parcels. She was addressed as 'Madam'; and on the least occasion she travelled in a great palanquin, flanked by extremely pretty maidservants and attended by clerks of age and dignity.

Their eldest son, Mansuke, born to opulence, showed a precocious talent for wasting money. His surroundings were of course luxurious, and never, not even in childhood, had he been exposed to the slightest harshness. Unable to calculate daily-instalment loans (a family business), he looked at the account-book only to sign it. His choice of reading matter, though limited, was presumptuous: he cared only to pore over verses in the classical style. As he gazed at flowers, he selected

X. *Characters of Worldly Young Men:* 'A Spendthrift'

> One of the workmen at the upper right explains that their house-wrecking is
> to clear the ground for a ball-field. Near them, the young master entertains
> on the veranda of his own home; farther to the left, at an extraordinary
> party. As the host jots down prices ('Let me see . . .'), a jester cries, 'There

goes the cup-stand! Now for the pot!' And the prodigal son remarks, 'What a delightful novelty!' Below, the boatmen marvel at this open-handed amusement: 'Nothing stingy about clearing the table that way!' 'I wish *I* could afford it!'

rhymes for Chinese poems; enjoying a snowfall, he boiled water for the tea ceremony. He tore down a back-garden house, which had been rented, and made a ball-field; and when he was playing *kemari* at the end of the day, he coveted Lu Yang's spear. He distributed dishes of rice and red beans throughout the neighbourhood to celebrate being listed on the honour roll at the light-archery range. During the intervals between morning and evening sports he kept busy with dissipation in the Shimabara.

One day, returning from a *nō* rehearsal at Ryōzen, Mansuke stopped at the Monji in Gion. The jesters who usually entertained him had no sooner heard of his arrival than they gathered round, unbidden, and offered one enticement after another. A jester called Foxy Denshichi made an especially deep bow. 'Recently', he said, 'I took over a lodging-house on the bank of the Takase River, and turned it into a restaurant. If you'll be so kind as to pay a visit on your way back, sir, though I'm afraid it's awfully shabby, the reputation of entertaining you will ensure its success.' Mansuke, happening to be in an excellent humour, replied that he would make a party of it, and take along all the girls. Immediately everyone in the group, without exception, decided to join him.

The manager greeted them with profuse hospitality. 'It is a great privilege', he said, 'to welcome you to the house of Denshichi.' Tapping his stick, he ordered all sorts of delicacies, and went to call in still other courtesans in honour of the occasion.

But the young master was not pleased. 'These borrowed furnishings of a new establishment!' he remarked distastefully. 'What a hideous cup-tray! Can't you have them replace everything?' Whereupon Hare-brained Kyūko, who had been sitting in a stiff, formal position, suddenly threw an awkwardly placed soup-bowl into the river flowing by the restaurant. His patron found this diverting. 'Better yet,' he said casually, 'toss the cup-tray in. A delightful idea!'

Kyūko, with the air of having made an important discovery, was about to throw the tray in, too, when their startled host came running out of the kitchen. 'I've just borrowed these things from the owner of the house', he cried angrily. 'What kind of behaviour is this, for a man of your age?'

His patron glanced coolly at him. 'Borrowed or not, if I pay for them there shouldn't be any objection. I enjoyed seeing that bowl float away, and doubt that you've any better entertainment for us. You may add it to the bill, so let him launch a few more.'

'In that case, sir,' the host replied, being experienced and alert, 'since you'll meet the cost of the articles, as you say, please throw out whatever you like, down to the house itself. Pick up anything at all—let's clear out these furnishings in a hurry! This is a novel pastime indeed!' He folded a piece of paper together to make a register and drew up an ink-stone. 'Five shingle-trays,[1] price, one *ryō* in gold', he called out. 'Ah! It's down in the book—gone! gone!'

Untouched by fears of guilt or retribution, everyone joined in the fun of hurling things into the river. The manager wrote down his estimates, which happened to be double the value of the articles. 'Ten of these red-patterned plates, 215 *momme* of silver; a *sake*-warmer, fifty-nine *momme*; nine wooden pillows, three *bu*, two *shu*; a willow chopping-board, bought yesterday and not one sardine cut up on it yet, yours for eighty-six *momme*; a hundred pairs of cedar chopsticks, twenty-three *momme*; a Yūji *sake*-cup,[2] two *ryō* in gold; a tobacco-tray with five pipes, one *ryō*, one *bu*; a rice tub, sixty-five *momme*; a wooden pestle, at eight *momme*; three ladles, ten *momme*; a lady's comb-box, tooth-blacking, and complete cosmetics set, all together, five *ryō*, one *bu*, four *momme*, and five *fun*. . . . Well, that's all—the only thing left is the picture-mounting opposite you, sir. While I'm putting these down, why not throw in the belongings of the midwife next door as well?'

At this, all the jesters spoke up together. 'Let's throw out your coin-purse, where you put the tips you get from your customers.'

They snatched at it, but he resisted and said, 'Spare me this!'

'Oh, you won't because there's a *bu* treasured up in it? But just add one to the master's bill, and it'll come to the same thing. For people of our sort a coin-purse is like a fine gentleman's storehouse. It'll spoil the party if we don't see it drift away.' The more reluctant he was, the more they enjoyed pressing him for it.

But Denshichi clapped his hands and said, 'Why not admit it holds the twenty-three family pawn-tickets, so it's bad luck to talk about letting things "drift away"! [3] He gets nervous at the very thought!' There was a roar of laughter, and they settled down to serious (though not sober) drinking.

After Mansuke had been helped into his sedan chair and promptly escorted homeward, the manager said, 'Well, this was a happy accident.' Counting it up on his abacus, he found that the sum of money so quickly realized came to fifty-three *ryō*, two *bu*, and two *shu*. While he was gratefully ringing the bell before the image of the God of Wealth, a cook and a man-servant returned from Matsubara carrying all his possessions, well soaked, between their shoulders. In fact, as soon as his guests had hit on the idea he had stationed men downstream with orders to retrieve everything, to the last chopstick. Now he learned that the price set down in his register was sheer profit—and obtained without even moistening his palms.

Who can keep self-indulgence from routing self-control, at least once in a lifetime? But when a young man, restrained by the gods and Buddhas, has the good fortune to turn from worldly pleasures midway in their course, sell all but his house, and throw himself into work making a living with a small stock of merchandise—when this happens, everyone from the people of the neighbourhood to the most distant relative forgives him, excusing his former conduct as youthful folly.[4] Yet things are by no means certain to turn out so well. Most young men are urged on by the God of Poverty till their circumstances become quite impossible. Then they announce: 'My profligate days are over'; but the coins they scattered never come rolling back. It takes no deep knowledge of the world to see that those who continue a life of pleasure, after swearing to die rather than beg, will certainly live to regret it.

Mansuke, perceiving that his father's severity was the mask of lenience, said that he had only spent two or three thousand *ryō* and didn't care to hear a noisy scolding. He decided to spare himself further rebuke by using some trickery to teach his father a lesson. He made a foil-covered wooden sword, and borrowed a religious charm [5] from the grandmother of a sedan-chair bearer named Nihei; these, together with two shrouds and a string of prayer-beads, he placed in a carrying-box,[6] which he closed and sealed. Slipping gold into the hand of the maidservant Kume, he drew her into the plot to falsify his condition, and he had rice balls hidden upstairs in the ladies' dressing-room. For four or five days he never left the house. When a meal was presented to him from time to time, morning, noon, or night, he would look at it with a wry face, and leave it untouched, saying, 'Anyway, I don't feel like eating.' Then he would hurry upstairs and devour the hoarded rice balls, thus keeping secure the fortress of his stomach. All food offered him was left uneaten, as if it had been set down before a Buddha or a courtesan.[7] He wore an air of anxiety, punctuated now and then by a distracted yawn. Even if there was something funny he made a heroic effort to suppress his laughter.

When his mother noticed this change, which was obvious enough, she at once sent for the seamstress Nui and the maid Kume, and began to question them piteously. 'I can't understand what's wrong with Mansuke these days. Has he complained of anything?'

'Not a word, Madam!' they replied in chorus. 'Still, he won't eat a bite for breakfast, lunch, or dinner, and when no one is looking he weeps and weeps. . . .'

'How cruel not to have told me!' the poor woman broke in. 'No artist could paint a son finer than Mansuke. All the master worries about from morning till night is to make more money to give him—if he's been grumbling at him for spending a little, it's only because he loves the boy and doesn't want his estate to dwindle away. Anyhow, starving himself like that will ruin his health. So first of all, please get him to eat more—be sure to give him his favourite dishes.' A son indifferent to such maternal distress ought surely to have lost divine favour, and to have been punished on the spot.

The maid, being in collusion with Mansuke, replied a little derisively: 'He mutters to himself, "Why should a man eat, except to sustain life?" So I don't think he'll take food, no matter what I serve him. If I tell you this, Master Mansuke may scold me for talking out of turn, but the fact is that a carrying-box—sealed, and handled as if it's important—has been stored away in his room. I feel suspicious about it.'

'How disturbing!' cried the mother, and rushed to Mansuke's room. When she broke open the box and looked into it she was horrified to see a complete outfit for double suicide. 'These days *shinjū* [8] is all the rage', she told his father. 'Didn't a rice-dealer's son die at Kōjin-gawara? And at Karasaki Beach there was the daughter of a screen-maker; and others at Mount Toribe, Gion Forest—many have died, in all sections, and the names are on everybody's lips. There's no doubt that that's what he means to do!'

The old man was alarmed, since (being out of step with the times) he was unacquainted with the tricks by which children extort money. 'Besides all the notoriety, it would be the ruin of the house', he reflected. 'If it's for some woman he's in love with, she's probably the wrong sort; but he means more to me than life itself, so I'll arrange it at once.' He asked his chief clerk to look into the matter; and Mansuke, when consulted, replied that he wanted to buy out a first-rank courtesan named Hanazaki, to make her his own.

The old man granted this request. 'I suppose it's happened before', he said, counting out a thousand *ryō* in *koban*.[9] 'Beat the price down as far as you can, and then pay it.'

Really, for a fake suicide, it was quite successful!

A SWAGGERER

Here, a shopkeeper's son follows the Way of the Samurai—and gets into trouble. Publicly disowned for the security of the neighbourhood, he suffers misfortunes which are entirely his own fault ('rust from the blade itself'). Yet his disobedience is unexpectedly rewarded.

THE astute tradesman will not veil a pious desire for the after-world. He knows that by telling his beads ostentatiously he may contrive to mingle self-interest with holiness.

Now a certain dealer in clerical wear, one who would have been happy to outfit the blackest demons,[1] kept such a modish shop that his robes and scarves sold briskly. As time went on he opened branches in Edo and Osaka, and gradually became quite rich. Yet (for all his money) he had the misfortune that he lacked an heir. Hoping to strike a bargain with Fate, he made elaborate vows to the gods and Buddhas.

Presently he was granted a son. He of course reared the boy with far more than ordinary care, and would gaze at him as rapturously as at flowers or the moon. He celebrated his son's coming of age at sixteen, gave him the name 'Jinshichi', and sent him round to wholesalers, and to the land-owning temples which were good clients of the shop. 'What a fine, handsome young man!' the proud parents said, forgetting all their avaricious dreams. Their one thought was 'Oh, for a girl worthy to be his bride!' They repeated his name as tenderly as if he were still an infant, and their love for him seemed boundless.

But Jinshichi was fond of military arts unsuitable to a shop-keeper. He made a wooden horse for home practice, and arranged to study horsemanship with a certain *rōnin* (a very skilful equestrian) who gave lessons near the Chion-in gate. Morning and night he practised riding, and he learned a precious secret technique of handling the reins. After that came training in other military skills. He had the sitting-room floor stripped of its mats; every day he summoned clerks and errand-boys to fence with him, using bamboo swords. All work was halted, while this art was pursued with the utmost diligence. Sometimes he put up a straw target and tried his hand at archery. As his conduct grew more and more extreme, he ordered a helmet and a suit of mail from an armourer on Gokō-machi, and displayed his braided armour in a large alcove. His unswerving aim was to behave like a samurai: nothing—not even stepping into a hot bath—could persuade him to leave his sword out of reach.

When he read books on strategy he expressed scorn for the troop dispositions carried out by famous commanders. 'They call Shingen of Kai [2] a great general,' he would begin, 'a man of sound judgment, courageous, resourceful, and all that. But wasn't he careless in the battle of Kawanaka-jima in Shinano? He relied on Yamamoto Kansuke, and only glanced over at Kenshin's position on Mount Saijō. No defences were set up by the river, so Kenshin bridged it in the night and defeated him. I'm not saying what would have happened if *I* had been there—but there's no doubt I'd have taken the head of "Kenshin, the bravest general in Etchū and Echigo". It's my greatest regret!' Thus he would talk, rubbing his arms conceitedly; while the father, since it was his beloved son, pretended not to notice.

Soon, though, this outrageous conduct exhausted the old man's patience. He came to the front room and sent for Jinshichi. 'You're not likely to get a fief,' he scolded, 'so it's nonsense to waste your time playing soldier. What's more, our line happens to be clerical garments, and that means doing business with priests. If you read Buddhist works instead, you could please a bishop by entertaining him with your conversation. Then one of them might take a seven-panel scarf, or a streamer for a holy banner. Now put a stop to your *jūjutsu* and fencing, and concentrate on getting orders for scarves and robes!'

When his father finished this harsh counsel and went back to the inner room, Jinshichi watched him go out and then called over a young clerk. 'Did you notice how I was sitting just then?' he asked. 'Besides giving advice, a testy old fellow like that might take it into his head to brandish a weapon—if only his pipe. So I twisted my body into a posture that gave me three parts strength, and my father six parts weakness. In that position you're quite invulnerable, even if somebody tries to hit you in the face. It's a useful trick called "thwarting a blow", one of Huang Shih Kung's [3] secrets. You observe how powerfully I can exert my will!' Thus a warning delivered with knitted brows and an air of deep concern had made not the slightest impression on him. Taking pride only in military skills, he grew more and more violent in his behaviour.

The more the old man thought about it the more frightened he became (despite his weakness for the boy), till he could no longer sleep at night. 'They call it the height of a young man's folly to be infatuated with harlots, and go chasing after young actors. But these only lead to the danger of losing money, perhaps at last a whole fortune. With my son Jinshichi, you can't tell what bloody deed he may do tomorrow, to put a noose around his old father's neck.'

After that his anxiety never ceased, and he finally asked the men of the neighbourhood to speak to Jinshichi. But his son lashed out scathingly at these kind neighbours, who had given him counsel for his own benefit. 'How wretched to enjoy the rare gift of human form, so difficult to obtain, and then end your days as a shopkeeper! What's the use of being born into this world? If that's all, I'm not one who would listen if the Buddha himself came down to give a long-winded, forty-nine-year sermon. No, the black robes we deal in may turn white, or my wooden horse sprout horns and gallop away—but a real man wouldn't think of dropping a resolution, once it's made. The virtue of being steadfast is a basic principle among men of character. I may come from the vulgar shopkeeping class, but I want to be a general instead. Don't make the insolent suggestion that the Way of the Samurai is "bad for business"!'

The neighbours and their leader, thinking it hopeless to argue with a fool who was match for a thousand, gave up and went to the old man. 'Master Jinshichi is your own dear son, but if you want to keep him we'd like both of you please to move to another neighbourhood. As long as that captain of the idiots is living here there's no telling when there'll be some calamity, to bring suffering on the whole group. Even if you privately disinherit him it may not keep your family out of trouble. Please consider the matter thoroughly.'

Since everyone at the local office seemed to agree on this, the old man submitted, and tried to reconcile his wife to the

XI. 'A Swaggerer'

Right: Two shop-boys hold sticks overhead and cry, 'If you insist, sir!'
And their young master, in samurai dress, shouts, 'Come on! Attack me!'
Sitting in the background is his fencing teacher. Left: The unfilial son's

moment of triumph. 'Shall I tame it for you?' he inquires, as the trampled grooms yell 'Ouch!' and the samurai beams down from the veranda: 'Wonderful!'

separation. 'It won't be so sad,' he told her, 'if you think of it as the time before we had a child.'

So Jinshichi was publicly disowned. He left his parents' house with only a short sword—coated with rust from the blade itself. For twenty-five *momme* and five *fun* he bought a crumbling hovel near Fushimi; and there he lived alone, barely able to survive by carving pivots for folding-fans. A frail wisp of smoke, morning and evening, rose from his kitchen fire. He spent the summer nights without a mosquito net, and he endured the winters without a blanket.

One day, after three years and three months, a *daimyō* from the western provinces happened to be passing. In his train there was a magnificent horse, led by seven or eight stable-boys. It was obviously a great treasure. Just at that moment, startled by something or other, the horse gave a bound, knocked over its keepers, and galloped off at amazing speed. Then it pranced into a dilapidated farm-house, terrifying an old woman, a mother, and her children. One after another the stable-boys ran up and tried to check it, but without success. When they were almost exhausted, Jinshichi stepped forward and said, 'If you'll allow me, I'll be glad to mount that animal and quiet it for you.'

At this, a man of samurai rank came over and glared at him. 'That "animal"', he announced in a withering tone, 'was named Yokoyama-chestnut because he's like the wild stallion that even Oguri Hangan could barely control.[4] He's my master's prized possession, and there are only one or two men in the whole clan who can ride him. For a peasant like you to say you'll tame him is the height of impudence. Suppose we let him make a meal of you if you can't?'

'By all means. If I fail, please do as you like with me.' He tucked the skirts of his wadded kimono in at the waist, as the horse approached. Suddenly he mounted it, thrust his feet firmly into the stirrups, and grasped the reins in the secret way he had learned. As he drew it under control, the horse—fierce as it was—became gentle and docile. Greatly impressed, the samurai hurried to report it to his lord.

When his attendants told him about the incident, the *daimyō* said, 'Let me know if that man will enter my service.' Gratefully, Jinshichi took a ceremonial position before the palanquin and was immediately granted an audience. Though the acquaintance had been short, he was permitted to enter into the compact between lord and vassal. He received the name Chestnut Jinshichi and at once set off for his new master's province.

Jinshichi pleased the *daimyō* more and more, and realized his ambition of acquiring a substantial fief. Thus a long-held interest in military matters was turned to profit.

A PRIG

In this sketch, appropriate as to moral if in somewhat doubtful taste, Kiseki takes up the seemingly harmless affectation of Chinese-style learning. Scholarship is often merely one of those polite accomplishments (like the tea ceremony) that may easily be carried to extremes. Here, the young man has a misplaced sense of filial piety, along with a knack of quoting Confucius to confound his elders. And Kiseki implies that most Confucianists are tireless, supercilious bores—Sinophiles who disdain not only Buddhism and the business-man's point of view but indeed all opinions except their own.

THE shrewd observer of the modern scene will note that sons are altogether inferior to their fathers, and that the grandson rarely offers hope for improvement.

First of all, people nowadays have lost the perseverance of their ancestors. But the ultimate secrets of an art or craft are not easily fathomed, even by the versatile. In medicine, for example, a man who has only the crudest training will wag his new-shaven head like a veritable sage, and will be sure that his long coat of pale blue silk-crêpe (which he feels to be suitably dignified) is set off with a short sword and a medicine box. He moves to a large town in a province where he is a stranger, displays his name on a huge placard at the gate-post, equips his house with an entrance in ornamental style, performs spectacular treatments, and the like. Yet a human being is invaluable, and the boundary between life and death has vital importance. The saying 'A doctor buries his mistakes' must refer to one of this sort.

Again, the tea ceremony is a Japanese custom that encourages social intercourse and leads to extravagance; the special merit of this art lies in faultlessness of detail. Today, a shopkeeper believes that whatever concerns the tea ceremony must be sumptuous: he will squander money on vessels and implements, reduce his business space to build a tea-room and a long pathway, train an epicure's palate, renew his wardrobe, and yearn for the exquisite in all things. Among the sophisticates of the capital a great many become homeless through this kind of luxury. Still, not to know how to conduct oneself is to be regrettably ill-bred. Even with a chipped tea-bowl, the purpose of the gathering is the same. At first, since this was the basis of the ceremony, one had only to learn the formalities—and grasp the spirit behind them—to enjoy this social pleasure entirely without strain. Yet now it is customary for a guest (who has been greeted with the utmost hospitality) no sooner to leave his seat than to begin disparaging the shapes of the charcoal and the placing of the flowers. Sufficient progress in this field for one to dare naming a tea-caddy would be difficult to achieve without at least ten years of training. And there are other skills on which each prides himself: writing linked-verses, arranging flowers, and performing solo dramatics, for instance. Who would be so rash as to drop an unstudied comment, in discussing them?

A learned man once declared: 'Such accomplishments as calligraphy, *kemari*, and singing immediately become known— after all, people have eyes and ears.[1] In particular, a young man lionized by society for his wealth will find that his other talents, however numerous, will be hidden by an awkward script. And scholarship is certainly the prime concern, after calligraphy, of anyone who wishes to become a superior person.'

These words, as it happened, were addressed to just such a young man. He at once abandoned all the many arts and skills which he had been pursuing. Hastily providing himself with books, he went to study under a *rōnin* Confucianist.

As soon as the young man had nearly mastered the Four Books [2] (by rote, that is), he announced that he had begun to practise Confucianism, and in fact showed it to the very tip of his nose. He considered other people to be in error, paraded his own wisdom, and scorned Buddhism as a heresy. When he heard his father read the Sutras morning and evening, he asserted that all this talk of Heaven and Hell (the last word in stupidity) came from a pack of lies told by corrupt priests to earn their bread. His character was transformed overnight, and he adopted an extremely consequential air.

'Dear me!' a regular customer would exclaim, coming to borrow money. 'Even in this fine weather our young gentleman doesn't go out to amuse himself. I should think you'd feel pent up, just staying inside. Still, behind your back everyone praises your behaviour enormously—it's a model for all the sons in the neighbourhood!'

To this flattery he would make no reply, except to say, tilting his Chinese fan affectedly: 'It is written that "Fine words and insinuating wiles are seldom associated with Virtue." [3] People of your sort who make insincerity their guiding principle miss my true character—"two-faced" is the word for you. It would be a shame for the clerks to follow your example, so don't let me see you around here any more.'

And as he spoke a disturbing gleam would come into his eye; so that even old customers stopped visiting the shop, and hesitated so much as to pay their respects at Bon and the New Year. The house trade, which had been thriving, grew remarkably quiet. 'The young master's studies will ruin us', the clerks complained to his father. 'He's always talking about the Way of the Five Duties, but never thinks of his own duty to help in our business. It would be better for this house if he'd practise the abacus, instead of quoting Confucius by the hour.'

The old man nodded agreement, and sent for his son. 'It's a great mistake for you to neglect the Way of the Merchant, on the pretext of scholarship', he scolded, knitting his brows. 'Besides, do Confucianists teach their students to be out-and-out fools—to go to brothels in the evening, come home in the middle of the night, and give free rein to their drunken whims, waking up all the servants? What nonsense to "Read the *Analects* and be ignorant of the *Analects*!" Hereafter, give up your books—use your head to balance accounts!'

The son, maintaining his pedantic air, promptly replied: 'In the words of Confucius, "A father conceals the misconduct of his son, and a son conceals the misconduct of his father: Morality demands this." [4] Hence, for a son to conceal his father's guilt, and a father his son's—this is Natural Propriety in the relation of parent and child, as well as the acme of Human Feeling. To observe Propriety is to be Moral. You, however, in a flagrant breach of Propriety, have just now permitted a group of clerks to hear you expose your son's unfortunate addiction to visiting brothels. How can you call that being Moral?'

The old man was disgusted. 'Moral or moronic, that gibberish interferes with business. In plain language, get down to your abacus!' This was the precept he gave his son.

Now on one occasion the classics teacher told the young man, 'To quote Master I Ch'uan,[5] "Anyone who has been granted human life—of high rank or low—ought to be acquainted with the art of healing." The reason is that it would surely be a gross default of filial piety and compassion to put a sick parent or child in the hands of a bungling quack—being unaware, from one's own lack of medical knowledge, whether a physician is good or bad.'

When the young man returned home after hearing this, he immediately fitted out a handsome medicine box, for which he procured a rich assortment of drugs. To begin his practice [6] he used the servants—the apprentice Kyūsaburō, the maid Tama, and the others—as if they were scraps of waste paper; and he found as much pleasure in administering needless drugs or massaging bellies which were entirely without pain as in viewing the moon or flowers. Delighted that he made no charge for his services, they loudly acclaimed him an expert. Tenants, wives, and old women who frequented the house—all came to beg for treatment. The young man threw away the abacus he had been calculating on, and took pulses; he put aside business already undertaken, and compounded medicines. Neglecting the family trade, he gave his attention wholly to medical practice.

The next morning someone came to the shop at dawn. A clerk, thinking it might be an early customer, hurried out at once to ask, 'What can I do for you?'

'I been suffering from them pills he had me take yesterday', the visitor answered. 'I vomited, my feet got a chill, and I couldn't pass water. Let me have a different prescription—I'm not ready to go to the next world!'

At this point the wife of a man named Shichibei, a back-alley neighbour, made her appearance. 'The physic my husband took last evening made his bowels run, and gave him a terrible fever. All night long he paced the floor of our little room. He was well enough yesterday, but he raved about passing out *sake*-money to a couple of men at the Yakko tea-house. Near dawn he weakened till he hadn't the strength to turn over in bed. I didn't think a man could sink so fast. For heaven's sake, give him back his health!'

With that, she sat down in front of the shop and waited; but

XII. 'A Prig'

At the upper right a man kneeling by an account-book tells his son, 'Now get down to the abacus!' But the young man merely says, 'I've given up all the arts in favour of scholarship!' Around him lie books, a bamboo flute, a

The purely anecdotal tal...
the year-end business hol...
his blade-shaped coins (...
gay quarter of Osaka to...
And there is a significan...
houses at Yu-no-o Cliff.

A CERTAIN wealth...
ing. Keeping up...
koban at a fashionab...
force of actors and...
samisen they dranl...
promptu), and clap...
continued, and thei...
while his precious...
failed to turn Kasa...
one tea-house to an...
an hour, and then...
the party next doo...
danced about from...
all twenty-eight in...
the day, as many as...
the second, there w...
house, where he sta...
over ninety, beside...
all joining the dai...
accommodate then...
left to carry on un...

He had no rega...
himself saw a danc...
could be more am...
his home in the...
settled down with...
washing. Once he...
of stopping. He w...

broken *samisen*. Towards his desk, a shop-boy regretfully splits a drum-head. Below, the young master busily dispenses pills and powders (and ignores business). The woman with the child asks the crippled old man, 'Are you here for medicine too?' 'Certainly, certainly!' he replies.

just then a tenan
hand. 'How can :
miserable tenant!
'What kind of me
at a single dose?
children are killec
I'll see that he pa

The clerk felt sc
moment', he said
about it, and then
a remedy. For the

'A precious ch
voice rose till it cc
that a time to slee
wicked thing—fo
ing for amusemer

Her words rea
height of foolishr
bours, he promp
out of bed.

XIII. 'A Rake'

'On with the dance!' cries the *samisen*-player at the lower right; while the
courtesans and jesters (one with an inverted cup-stand as a funny hat) circle
into the next room and back ('Ah-h!' 'Hey!'). And the young rake sitting

before the folding screen exclaims, 'It's so delightful I can hardly bear it!'
(The scene at the left is from a different story, not translated, in which a
father encourages his son to visit the gay quarter—till he tires of it and wants
to go temple-visiting instead.)

other: everyone knew the name of Yoshinoya Shōgo. There is hope for a son who receives the proper advice. But since this young man had no one to worry about, he delighted in his freedom to squander money. He enjoyed all the advantages of a rich orphan. Unrestrained, unadmonished, he gave himself wholly to the pursuit of pleasure.

One day this dancing patron called together actors and jesters. 'An unfortunate matter has come up', he said, frowning. 'I'd like you to dip into your wits and suggest something.' He spoke meaningfully, in a low voice.

His hearers exchanged glances and began to calculate in their hearts. The end of the year was not far off, they reasoned, and so he would no doubt want his tea-house bills deferred till he raised some money. Silently they speculated. At last one of them said, 'In your case, sir, even if you fall behind once or twice there is certainly no one who'll press you. Don't give it a thought. Come! Are we ready?' Whereupon he clapped hands smartly, and plunged into a reckless dance.

But the young gentleman waved his fan for quiet. 'I haven't the slightest worry of that sort', he explained. 'As a matter of fact, I've paid enough money in advance to cover all next year's tea-house expenses. What I want your advice on is this: the other day Sakichi told me all the owners have asked us not to have any big parties from the twenty-fifth of the month to the third day of the New Year. They say everyone will be busy paying bills, and having so many guests would make it hard to balance accounts. Now that means we'll have to give up our dancing parties for a whole week, doesn't it? I can't help feeling upset. Isn't there any place where we can dance in the New Year without being bothered? Try to think of one!' He *did* seem disturbed.

Caught off guard by their master's wish, the jesters, who were at least volatile fellows, clapped their hands in surprise. 'Ah, indeed! How natural to worry! It's only for a short time, but it takes serious thought—we'll all join forces and work out some kind of plan. Please, sir, allow us to assure you there's no need for concern!' And they put their heads together and cudgelled their feeble brains, as if anxiously engaged in capping verses.

At this point an actor from the South quarter spoke up. 'It's curious,' he said, 'but I must confess that my better ideas don't come without a glimpse of gold.'

Unable to resist these rather broad hints, the rake called for his purse, which a retainer carried, and showered down golden blossoms till even the servant-girls going back and forth in Kasaya-machi received an unlooked-for bounty.

Then a jester named Shinshichi said, 'From the twenty-fifth to the third you can hire a large boat at Kawaguchi, and have any kind of party you want.'

But the actor Jōemon shook his head. 'The master can't stand boats. How about taking private rooms at the Tennō Temple?'

The reply 'You can't dance there at night' silenced him.

'Well, where shall we go?'

And each filled another soup-bowl of wine, drank, folded his arms, and pondered.

Finally, a jester called Wambako made a good suggestion. 'I've got it! The best spot in Japan for the kind of party you want, where nobody interferes! Next month, on the first, let's leave here and visit the hot springs at Arima. People go there all year round, no matter if it's Bon or the New Year—and as much for pleasure as for the cure. Whatever your tastes, they can be indulged handsomely any time. Now in the first place, it'll be amusing, for a change. Then, too, since all of us will escape the annual reckoning, we'll be quite carefree. Well, sir! A brilliant idea, isn't it? But it's near the end of the year, so I'll let you have it for a single *ryō*.' Even in yawning he gaped with greed.

'Splendid!' exclaimed the rake, suddenly cheerful again. 'Why not leave at once?'

Preparations for the trip were ordered immediately. Actors and jesters who were not engaged, tea-house owners who were short of funds to settle their accounts—at least eighteen or so set out together, to go all the way by sedan chair. Thanks to their patron, they would end the year without seeing the face of a single creditor. Grateful, and not merely for the beneficial waters of Arima, these quite healthy fellows had no sooner arrived than (omitting all the usual routine) they went to a second-floor reception-room and began a party.

Other guests, really ill, now lay on throbbing pillows, and grew angry at the return of headaches which they had been at some pains to cure. Still others, in more distant rooms, complained that their ears had begun to ring again.

The innkeeper was disturbed, and hurried upstairs. 'You gentlemen are dancing with marvellous vigour,' he said, 'but here there are invalids on all sides, and for some time now they have been suffering from your boisterousness. Never before has Arima had such high-spirited patients. Gentlemen, may I ask what sort of illness has brought you here to recuperate?'

The jester Shimbachi, always rather glib, said, 'Dancing is our disease. If we go into the water, we'll break out violently, won't we?'

But the innkeeper had the last word.

'In that case,' he replied affably as he rose to leave, 'I must beg you to try the special remedy at Yu-no-o Cliff.' [1]

A WORTHLESS TRIO

Of course Kiseki does not always let his scapegraces off with a spoiled holiday or a mere inconvenience. An omnibus Character of the three sons of a rich money-lender illustrates three altogether different temptations, and then shows, in the best cautionary style, what may come of indulging in them. Here as elsewhere the swift descent of cast-off sons brings in a ragged company of beggars, panders, and men who make a poor living in some more strenuous fashion. The fates of these three, at least, are determined by a strict poetical justice.

A CERTAIN man who was called 'Chief Creditor of the *Daimyō*' had an imposing mansion in the heart of the capital. As spokesman of the money-lending fraternity, he took the seat of honour at the Nisai Association. Day by day increasing his wealth, he served a superb clientele: the specialties of all the provinces of Japan came to him as gifts from their lords, who were his regular customers. Crested formal garments of the season [1] reflected the *Mirror of Edo* [2] from his clothes-racks; his scrolls of both Chinese and Japanese calligraphy and painting formed a huge collection, he had no idea how large; choice specimens of such wares as Yōhen, Kenzan, Ido, Mishima, Kohiki, and Komagai [3] were stacked and tied, and the number of boxfuls noted; celebrated tea objects were crammed into long chests. He owned antique gold-brocade coverlets and quilts, curtains of richly patterned brocade, a hundred badgers in solid gold, a hundred coral branches, a hundred silver bowls of the Temmoku shape, and a hundred pairs of tortoise-shell chopsticks—to say nothing of his stores of plain gold, silver, rice, and cash. There was no one in the capital to compare with him.

His three sons were reared in luxury. They were shallow-brained fellows, accepted as students only for their money; yet to the old man (who failed to observe how large they had grown) these clever children were a source of happiness. 'One day I'll retire and enjoy old age to the full', he thought.

But the eldest son, Magotarō, had meanwhile begun to

frequent the Shimabara. Night and day, never glancing aside, he came by three-man sedan chair, or rode in the Chinese-style boat [4] of the Ichimonji-ya. In his wild revels he passed through many experiences. And besides being good-looking, as well as devoted to pleasure, he made it a habit to give his smart clothes the fragrance of precious incense, and to cultivate a manner of studied elegance, most attractive to women. Yet this handsome fellow, whom a courtesan of the highest rank would have gladly entertained at her own expense, had an un-limited supply of money; so that all the girls lost their hearts to him, and he tasted the ultimate delights of love. 'Even in India there may be no such joys', he thought, as he squandered money in sums larger than he troubled to count.

Deeply disturbed, his father had the chief clerk give the boy a sound moral lecture. But familiarity with courtesans had taught his eldest son to be glib. 'My father', he declared, 'has no idea of how much is enough. He's already the first or second richest man in the capital, and now he's greedier than ever. In the morning he gets up while the stars are out, and goes in tradesman's dress to do business with the stewards of the great houses. He undertakes to carry out huge exchanges, and shortens his life by worrying till they're settled; or he struggles to accumulate vast sums of money, and then, blinded by his desire for high interest, hands them over to perfect strangers. But in this world it's hard to get payment on the terms of a house mortgage; and a scrap of paper won't turn into money, no matter how you twist it. Wouldn't it be better to let his own son have at least enough to amuse himself? This is what you call parental benevolence. Besides, I'm sure that what *I've* spent doesn't add up to the worthless notes in *his* strong-box.'

Thus, instead of accepting a little advice, he complained that his allowance was too small. Since the son seemed unwilling to give up his excesses, the father, out of desperation, called a family council. At last Magotarō was quietly disinherited, and put in seclusion under a priestly guardian at Mii Temple.[5] But a charred post is easily set afire. He became a habitual visitor to Shibaya-machi,[6] the nearest pleasure quarter, and waded up to his neck in the lake of passion.

In view of this scandalous behaviour, the old man decided to have his second son, Magojirō, become his representative to the great houses. Summoning him, he announced this intention.

Now Magojirō bore no resemblance whatever to his hand-some elder brother. He was dark-skinned and tall, with knotty muscles and thick-jointed limbs. From childhood he had been proud of his strength, delighting in *jūjutsu* and *sumō*. He wrestled with local strong-men at country festivals (not to mention temple charities), and boasted that he had never suffered defeat. He wore a loin-cloth of figured silk; his appetite was constant and indiscriminate; his arms were tattooed so thickly that the skin looked like one of those fabrics printed in char-acters; and his forehead was high and bald, like that of Miken-jaku.[7] He would seize servants or errand-boys, and throw them; and he announced himself as 'Rough-waves Magoji, well known through all these provinces'. Uprooting the willows of the *kemari* field at their other mansion, he built a row of *sumō* rings. For even a modest entertainment he called in wrestlers. 'This is the only pleasure in life', he said; and he devised catches beyond the forty-eight standard ones, never caring whether the lords' money had been won or lost, so long as he won at wrestling. Nothing else received the faintest attention from him.

As a result the old man would frown, and deliver one scold-ing after another. 'Anyone', he would say, 'might expect a person in your circumstances to be fond of the *koto*, chess, calli-graphy, and painting, and to be interested in such things as the tea ceremony, *kemari*, light archery, and the *nō* drama. But leaping naked into dangerous wrestling bouts! Is that what you call right conduct for the heir to a house that lends to the great lords? Now put a stop to it, and amuse yourself properly!'[8] But the young man merely insisted that *sumō* was the only pleasure in life. There was no reason to think he might abandon it.

His father and mother, after consulting with the whole family, decided that if they could at least hasten his marriage, and get a fascinating wife for him, there would doubtless be a natural change in his attitude. So they arranged a match with the daughter of a dry-goods merchant on Nakadachiuri, and the marriage ceremony was happily concluded. But Magojirō never entered the girl's room. His parents rubbed their heads

XIV. 'A Worthless Trio'

Magojirō stands among his wrestling cronies at the lower right ('Women disgust me!' 'Take the maids back into the house!'); while on the veranda the third son Magosaburō, begging for praise, manipulates a puppet in a spear dance. His *go*-board platform stands before the regular stage. A *samisen*-player and a *jōruri*-reciter assist him, as the family tradesmen obedi-

ently look on. At the upper left he appears in night-kimono among his puppets—shouting 'Ladies and gentlemen!' Below, his handsome elder brother Magotarō (who also wears the family crest) is about to set off for another party. The girls are giving him his coat, sword, and medicine box ('Hurry! the *tayū*'s waiting!'). But an attendant wants to see what is going on over the wall.

in wretchedness. When they had the matter brought up by the wet-nurse, who had come in attendance on the bride, Magojirō changed colour and asserted: 'Sleeping with women saps a man's strength in the prime of life, and he can't wrestle. By the gods of Atago and Hakusan,[9] even if I burned with passion I wouldn't touch a woman!' His unfortunate bride was desolate, a widow though her husband still lived. She was left to wait [10] alone morning and evening at the door of the bedchamber. Magojirō, obsessed with the joys of *sumō*, became more and more fond of meat-eating; he grew so sturdy in bone and muscle that at twenty-three he seemed to be thirty-four or thirty-five, and his appearance was completely changed.

Since the old man decided that such behaviour made him unfit for serving the *daimyō*, he disowned his second son too, and turned him out. At a private conference with the clerks everyone agreed that the third son, Magosaburō, should be made head of the house; and they tried to prepare this boy to represent the family.

Unlike his elder brothers, Magosaburō neither visited the gay quarter nor devoted himself to feats of strength. However, since childhood he had been fond of giving puppet shows. In his own eight-mat room he put up a rail and hung a gold brocade curtain, just as in an actual theatre. He bought a great many puppets made by Heiji and dressed them in all sorts of costumes, of printed fabrics and cloth of gold.[11] He had the neighbourhood hairdresser recite *jōruri* and had a blind begging-woman (who came regularly) play the *samisen*. The apprentices of the family fishmonger, greengrocer, and bean-curd-dealer were summoned to make up the audience. He was like a child—even at an age when he might have been helping his father drum up business, the young idiot would beat his own drum wildly and cry, 'It's beginning! It's beginning!' From morning till night he danced and jumped about, manipulating his puppets. Every day was like Bon or the New Year, in his enthusiasm for this diversion. At night he would burn candles in order to copy a plot or rehearse his puppets in a fresh *jōruri*. Thus we see fools of all kinds.

How pitiful that a man with three outstanding sons should be unable to find a worthy heir among them! At last he had to adopt one from another branch of the family; and he turned his back on his own three, refusing to let them come near him.

Magotarō, the eldest, had a hard time getting along in the outside world, and began to traffick in low prostitutes in Miya-gawa-chō. 'My father certainly has a heart of stone', he complained. 'Anyway, I'm sure the clerks will become my patrons, and bring their business here.' The roles were reversed, as he talked like a jester and addressed servants (whom he now served), with 'Look, Master!' He had a real lap-dog as his only sycophant, and a shop-worn whore as his wife. Remembering the splendours of the past, he showed his new wife how to promenade in the manner of the famous beauty Morokoshi,[12] and he enjoyed having her behave like a courtesan.

In the meantime the next younger brother, Magojirō, having ignored a whole series of warnings to give up *sumō*, had finally been tripped by his father and thrown out of the house—even before being thrown out of the ring. He realized that, however skilful, he was no match for the old man. Though he begged forgiveness, this champion was allowed to come no nearer than the gate; and as he sat there the strength he had been so proud of slowly ebbed. Since he knew no one to turn to, he could only support himself by selling his clothes. At last he was next to naked, but then a carter noticed his tattered damask loin-cloth [13]—kept for sentimental reasons—and hired him out of admiration for his love of wrestling. Thus the wheel [14] of fortune, having brought him to this state, turned; and he ended his days in Shimotoba.

Because hand-puppets were what Magosaburō, the third son, had indulged in with such wilful extravagance, he was useless in ordinary marionette theatres, and could find no employment. After operating a mechanical doll theatre for a while (as his own fortunes were running down), he landed a job as gate-keeper at a peep-show. 'Come, now!' he would shout hoarsely. 'You can pay on your way out!'

This was the notorious half-wit called 'Third-son Mago-saburō'!

From

The Woman Who Spent Her Life in Love

by Ihara Saikaku

THE WOMAN WHO SPENT HER
LIFE IN LOVE

Of Saikaku's twenty-four chapters, ten are here translated in full. These ten chapters include many of the highlights of his rambling confessional tale. Selected neither to expurgate nor to underline its ribaldry, they follow it from the flowery beginning, in which the author explains how he happened to eavesdrop at the 'Hermitage of Voluptuousness' as the old woman told her story, through most of the early and a few later episodes of her pungent reminiscences. The final chapter brings her confession to its rather equivocal end. Ironically, the heroine has done her scandalous bit to bring men to sainthood, by helping them extirpate their passions. The opening proverb has indeed set the tone of the entire tale: a burlesque variation on the Buddhist theme shogyō mujō ('All is vanity').

AN OLD CRONE'S HERMITAGE [1]

To quote the ancients, 'A beautiful woman is an axe that chops off life.'[2] The blossoms of the heart are scattered; by evening the tree itself has been turned to firewood. Who can escape? As for those who venture out into an unseasonable morning tempest, drown in lust, and die young—how very stupid of them! Yet their kind is by no means rare.

Early on the seventh day of the first moon, as I was going to Saga, west of the capital, I crossed the Umezu [3] River. The plum flowers were opening, as if to say 'Spring is here!' Just then I noticed a pair of young men, one of whom was handsome, fashionably dressed, but extremely languid. He looked pale, worn out by love. His future seemed so unpromising that his parents would surely soon become his heirs. But he spoke of a sole desire: 'I, who have lacked for nothing, wish only that love's elixir flowed as inexhaustibly as this river.'

His companion was startled. 'My own wish', he said, 'is for a country without women. I'd go there and lead a completely idle life, and a considerably longer one, observing the endless variety of this changing world.'

Their ideas on life and death could hardly have been more

different. Still, short as life is, they went on pursuing their unfulfilled dreams, and talking about them vacantly together.
Dizzy with such perverse thoughts, they groped their way
down a path that ran along the bank of the river. Trampling
blindly through budding shoots of thistle and wild parsley, they
hurried on into the recesses of the northern mountains, away
from the village.

When I followed them, curious to know where they were
going, I came at last to a clump of red pines and a sparse fence
of withered *hagi* [4] branches with a gate of plaited bamboo-
grass and a rough hole for a dog to go through. Inside, there
was a natural rock-cave, a peaceful shelter protected by a
sloping roof. Ferns drooped from the eaves, and the ivy still
kept its past autumn foliage. Water, carried by bamboo pipe
from a clear spring, trickled out under a willow to the east. 'No
doubt some pious recluse lives here', I thought; but I was
astonished to find a woman. Though not without an air of
refinement, she was old and bent, her hair lay in frosty strands,
and her eyes were as dim as the light of a setting moon. She
wore an old-fashioned wadded-silk garment of sky-blue, dotted
with double chrysanthemums in white. Her sash, which bore a
pattern of lozenges, was of medium width—and tied in front! [5]
Such an outfit, at her age! Still, the effect was not too bad.

On a plaque of weathered wood, hung over the moulding of
a room that appeared to be her bedroom, there were inscribed
the words 'Hermitage of Voluptuousness'. A thin fragrance—
probably of the celebrated incense called Hatsune—lingered
in the air. While I peered through a window, my heart ready to
leap through it, I saw the two men walk in as if they knew
exactly where they were.

The old woman beamed at them. 'Gentleman-guests even
now!' she exclaimed. 'But why come here, like the wind in a
dead tree, when other women could give you a much better
time? Since I'm hard of hearing and slow in talking, I have
trouble getting along with people these days. I've spent the last
seven years shut up in this place. The blossoming plum tree is
my spring almanac; when the green mountains are buried in
white, I know it's winter. I never see so much as a stray visitor
any more. How does it happen you've come to call on me?'

'My friend is tortured by love,' replied one of them, 'and I

XV. Hambei: *The Woman Who Spent Her Life in Love*: 'An Old
    Crone's Hermitage'

    The 'Hermitage of Voluptuousness' in its woodland setting. The old woman

plays the *koto* as one of her gentlemen-guests accompanies her on the flute
. . . unaware that they are being watched. Her kimono has a gaudy pattern
of double chrysanthemums.

am perhaps overly fond of it, but have yet to learn its ultimate secrets. We heard about you and came, so please tell us the un-varnished story of your life.' Pouring a drop of *sake* into an exquisite gold wine-cup, he urged her to drink.

Before long the old woman got a little tipsy. She began to play the *koto*, evidently her constant pastime, and sang a few snatches of a romantic ballad. Then, rapt, overwhelmed by emotion, she poured out all the many passions and vicissitudes of her life:

I was born into a good family. My mother certainly had nothing to boast of, but my father's ancestors were intimate with members of the Court nobility . . . in the time of the Emperor Go-Hanazono.[6] Of course the family had declined since then; as a matter of fact we were completely down and out. But since I happened to be graceful, and a natural beauty, I went into the service of a Court lady who was held in the highest favour at the Palace. This elegant life suited me very well, and after serving the usual length of time I would doubt-less have had a splendid position in society.

But early in the summer of my eleventh year I began to feel strangely restless. The way people did my hair bored me, so I insisted on a 'hanging Shimada' with the back hair drawn in, tied smartly by a hidden cord. I became extremely particular in my tastes. The reason the 'palace-style' of print came into vogue was that I worked from morning till night to design new patterns.

The whole way of life of the Court nobles—even their game of *kemari* and the nature of their poems—stimulated my amorous tendencies. Seeing only people who spent their time in and out of bedrooms gave me giddy notions; so did hearing them talk about it. Naturally my feelings were entirely wrapped up in the pursuit of love—and just at that time I began to receive all sorts of love-letters, each pathetically saturated with emotion. Later, running out of storage space, I asked one of the less talkative guardsmen to send them up in empty smoke. All those inextinguishable vows pledged before the myriad deities had to flutter back to the Yoshida Shrine.[7]

What is so queer as love? Many fine, handsome gentlemen made advances to me—and left me cold. Obviously I wouldn't care for a green young samurai, the unimportant retainer of an important person. Still, one of them wrote me letter after letter, as passionately as if he would give his life for me. Before I knew it I had fallen painfully in love.

Cleverly arranging a rendezvous, I yielded my body to him. At last people began to talk, but I couldn't let him go. And early one morning we were surprised together. I was punished by being sent back where I came from, near the Uji Bridge,[8] but alas! the young man really did give his life for me. The next four or five days, as I lay sleepless, half out of my senses, he appeared to me again and again, never saying a word. It was so horrible I thought of killing myself. But the days passed and I forgot all about him. You know how shamefully fickle women are. Of course I was only thirteen at the time, so people were indulgent. Some of them said, 'Surely not at her age . . .'. That amused me.

Formerly, young ladies going off to marry wept at the farewell, drenching their sleeves in tears. Nowadays a girl is more knowing. Impatient with the go-between, she hurries to get ready, jumps into the sedan chair (which she has eagerly awaited), and radiates joy from the very tip of her nose. Till forty years ago a girl of even eighteen or nineteen could be found playing at her gate, riding a bamboo hobby-horse; a boy would as a rule be initiated into manhood at twenty-five. How quickly times have changed!

I, too, was steeped in love, as the yellow rose is steeped in its colour, when I had only begun to bloom. Plunging into the Rapids of the Roses,[9] I let myself be swept away to ruin. There was no way for me to stem the current.

MUSICAL AND DANCING FESTIVITIES

PEOPLE who keep their ears open say uptown and down-town Kyoto differ in every way. When the light-blue flowered summer kimono begin to disappear, as flowers fade, you hear drums beating all over town and see the Komachi dance performed by little girls with pinned-up hair and hanging sleeves.[10] As far as Shijō the dancers are calm and graceful, in the true spirit of the capital. But below that, to the outskirts of the city, voices are strident and footsteps clatter. What a change!

When a girl has a sense of rhythm, and is on pitch enough to seem out of the ordinary, she can make a name for herself. During the Manji Era [11] a blind musician called Shuraku came down from Abekawa, in the province of Suruga, to Edo. For the amusement of the aristocracy he would play single-handed (and inside a paper mosquito-net) eight different musical instruments at once. Later he came to the capital where, be-sides introducing this art, he spent a great deal of time devising polite dances and music, in which he offered instruction. Young girls flocked to him, to learn this way of making a living. Don't think they were *kabuki* women! After their training, these lovely girls might go to attend ladies of the nobility for an evening's pleasure. Their costume was nearly always the same: an undergarment reverse-lined in red silk; a white wadded-silk kimono with a pattern in gold and silver leaf, the neckband black; a left-twisted, tricolour cord sash, tied at the back; to-gether with a short sword of gilt wood, a medicine box, and a purse. Some wore a boyish coiffure—partly shaved at the top and puffed out behind.

Their patrons would have them sing short ballads, dance, pour the *sake*, and afterwards bring in the soup. When country samurai or old gentlemen were entertained in Higashiyama the presence of five or six of these charming little girls would make the party a complete success. To spirited young men, however, they seemed a bit dull.

Their fee was set at one *bu* in gold each, which was modest enough. To look at them, they were simply pretty children of eleven, twelve, or thirteen. But they knew their business! Accustomed to the gentlemen of the capital, they could please men more skilfully than any little apprentice of the Osaka gay quarters. And as they grew older, at fourteen or fifteen, say, they no longer ended an evening by merely letting their guests go home. Not that they would dream of being crude about it . . . only they would behave coquettishly, as if they might easily be seduced. When a man warmed up to one of them she would slip adroitly out of his grasp—in order to tighten her grip on him. 'If you care for me,' she would say, 'come alone to my master's place, on the sly. Then, as soon as you get the chance pretend to be giddy from *sake* and go off to bed—but leave the young musicians a tip, so they'll make a great uproar to please you. We can take advantage of all the noise and excitement. . . .'

Thus the gentleman's feelings were deftly stirred. Through such expert manœuvring, visitors from the more remote provinces were fleeced of impressive sums. The average man was unaware of it, but all these girls were after the same thing. Even a well-known dancer could be had for a piece of silver.[12]

Now when I was still very young I often came in from Uji because, though I had no intention of joining them, I liked the style of these little girls. I learned all the latest fads, and became quite an excellent dancer. The more everyone sang my praises, the more I loved it. Paying no attention to those who warned me I would come to a bad end, I turned professional—and made quite a splash. Sometimes I appeared at splendid parties. But since my mother always came along I was never (unlike the other girls) guilty of the slightest misconduct. Men found it impossible to have me, which tormented them all the more. Some pined away entirely.

About that time a lady from the Western Provinces rented a place in Kawara-machi for her health. Not being so ill as to have to take medicine, she went out in a luxurious sedan chair every day—from the season of midsummer heat till that of snow in the northern mountains. Once, as she was going along the Takase River, her glance fell in my direction. And she took such an instant fancy to me that she arranged to have us meet. From morning to night she and her husband doted on me. They

XVI. 'Musical and Dancing Festivities'

Above the cloud-line, a glimpse of Kiyomizu Temple in Higashiyama, overlooking Kyoto. Below, a gentleman peeks through the wind curtain to see the

singularly beautiful dancing-girl performing at this gay party under the
cherry blossoms. A country samurai, followed by two servants, hurries up
from the right.

decided that in view of my behaviour, which was far from vulgar, I would not do badly as a wife for their only son, who had been left at home. So they adopted me, and I was assured a happy future.

Looking at her, you felt that this lady was uglier than any you saw in the capital—or in the country, for that matter. Yet her husband was so handsome that it would have been hard to find his equal, even at the present Court. Since they thought I was still too young to realize what was going on, they had me sleep with them. Of course I'd known all about that sort of thing for three years, so their frolics gave me an odd sensation. But I had to grit my teeth and bear it.

One night as I was lying awake, and rather lonely, I felt the touch of my master's leg. I forgot everything then, except to make sure that his wife was snoring soundly. Slipping into bed with him, I behaved as seductively as possible. Intent on love, we were quite unable to stop.

You can imagine how long that lasted.

'Yes, indeed! the capital is no place to be caught napping! In our part of the country a little girl like that would still be playing at her gate, riding a bamboo hobby-horse.'

Dismissed with a burst of laughter, I was again sent home to my parents.

PROVINCIAL LORD'S FAVOURITE

I T happened that one year a certain *daimyō* was in residence
at Edo, a city never disturbed by winds sighing among its
pines.[13] His wife had just died; and his retainers, deploring that
he lacked an heir, had seen to it that more than forty lovely
girls of decent family were stationed near his bedroom—ready
to go in whenever their wily mistress thought the time was ripe.
All of them were like budding cherry flowers which would
come into full bloom after being moistened by a single shower.
You would suppose that none could have tired the gaze.

Unfortunately, to the great distress of the household, not one
of these girls interested the *daimyō*. If you stop to think of it,
low-born women brought up in the East are known for being
ungainly creatures—invariably thick-necked, flat-footed, and
tough-skinned. They are shrewd but not amorous. Neither
grasping nor timid, they may be said to have hearts of gold;
still they scarcely make good sleeping-partners. When it comes
to women, have you heard of any place better than the capital?
For one thing, we have an incomparable charm of speech—
quite unstudied, but handed down as a palace tradition. Here
is an example of that influence. The men and women of
Izumo, 'where the eight clouds arise',[14] are often slovenly in
their way of talking; but the people of the still more distant
Oki Islands, though they have a rustic look about them, are
exactly like the people of the capital in their speech. They are
so refined that the women devote themselves to the arts of the
koto, chess, incense, and classical poetry. And all this is simply
because Prince Ninomiya [15] was exiled there long ago: in
everything the customs of that time have been preserved.

Naturally it was thought the capital would have something
choice.

Now there was one old fellow, past seventy, who had long
been in charge of the ladies' quarters of that household. He was
blind without his glasses, and so gap-toothed he'd forgotten the
flavour of octopus and even had to have his pickled vegetables

grated fine. His days were entirely empty of worldly pleasures —including of course the pleasures of sex. He had a man's loin-cloth, to be sure, but he might as well have been a woman: his only licentiousness came in talking about such things. Still, as a man performing the duty of a samurai, he wore formal military dress. Though not allowed to carry the usual pair of long and short swords, he was entrusted with what was suited to his feebleness: the key to the silver lock on the inner apartments. Having this man judge the Kyoto women was like leaving a stone Buddha with a cat [16]—no need to worry! Who would trust the Buddha himself, in his younger days, with articles of that kind?

So the old man came to a certain house called the Sasa-ya, among the dry-goods shops in the Muromachi quarter of the Heavenly Capital.[17] 'My present business cannot be discussed before the young clerks', he announced. 'I want a private con-ference with the old master and his wife.' Everyone wondered uneasily what he had in mind.

At last, looking very grave, he explained, 'I'm here to choose a concubine for my lord.'

'We've had these requests from all the *daimyō*', he was assured. 'Now just what sort would you like?'

Then the old fellow produced from a scroll box of straight-grained paulownia wood the painting of a beautiful woman. 'I'd like to engage one about like this', he said, to make clear his preference. And he added, as they looked at it: 'First of all, her age should be from fifteen to eighteen, and she should have the most up-to-date good looks—that is, the face slightly rounded, the complexion of a pale cherry-blossom, the four features all perfectly regular. Narrow eyes are not wanted; the eyebrows should be thick and spaced well apart on either side of the nose, which ought to stand fairly high. A small mouth; gleaming white teeth; longish ears, delicately rimmed and set far enough out to be completely visible. The forehead should have an unplucked, natural hairline; the nape of the neck should be slender, and free from any stray wisps of back hair. As for the fingers, long and slim, with thin nails. The length of the feet is fixed at size eight and three-tenths—the big toe curved so that you can see its underside. Her body should be taller than the average: the hips firm but not too well padded, the buttocks plump. She must know how to carry herself, and to dress well. Dignified in appearance, mild of disposition, she will excel in all the arts appropriate to a woman—and be thoroughly informed on them. Also, please, a girl whose skin is without a blemish.'

'The capital is vast and has an endless supply of women', they told him. 'Still, among all of them, there must be very few who would meet such exacting tastes. But if the lord of a province wishes it—and is prepared to offer a thousand pieces of gold— we'll find one if there's one to find!' And they gave this singular mission to Hanaya Kakuemon, of Takeya-machi, a procurer of long experience.

Now those who make a living by placing girls in this kind of service take ten *ryō* out of a hundred *ryō* in advance money. Again, out of the ten *ryō*, the old woman who acts as go-between takes ten *momme* in silver. Girls lacking a proper wardrobe can easily rent an outfit for the trial period: a white wadded-silk garment, or a kimono of figured black satin under one dotted in white all over, a wide Chinese-brocade sash, a scarlet silk-crêpe underskirt, a palace-style cloak—everything, down to the very cushions of the sedan chair, can be rented for twenty *momme* a day. When the girl is finally accepted, another piece of silver must be paid. A girl of extremely low birth is placed in the care of a poor shopkeeper (who is called her foster-father), and then sent out as his child. He profits by a gift from her master. If as time goes on she happens to present her master with an heir, her 'foster-father' may have the luck to get a steady rice-stipend.

When a girl wants to do as well as possible she finds it expensive. The rent for her wadded kimono will be twenty *momme*; for a sedan chair with two bearers, three *momme* and five *fun*— the same price to any point in the capital. A very young maidservant will cost her six *fun*, an older one eight *fun*; and their two meals a day will be at her expense. But after going to all this trouble she may fail to please, and so have lost twenty-four *momme* and nine *fun*. What a way to make a living!

Sometimes Osaka and Sakai merchants, when they aren't busy carousing at the Shimabara or the Shijō-gawara quarter, get the inspiration to dress up their silly jesters as rich men from the Western Provinces, and then amuse themselves by bringing

XVII. 'Provincial Lord's Favourite'

Two chair-bearers rest at the gate, an attendant kneels below the veranda, and the travel-worn heroine poses coyly before the delighted old samurai.

He wears formal costume and carries two swords, on this crucial mission for his *daimyō*.

together all the would-be mistresses in the capital. Keeping back the girls who manage to have caught their fancy, they quietly try to arrange a one-night term of duty. If a girl takes offence at this sudden turn of affairs, and wants to leave, she is talked down by arguments of all kinds—among which a sordid appeal to greed is the most effective. Inevitably she accepts a temporary bedfellow and sells her favours, complete, for two *bu* in gold. Of course a girl whose family is well off would never agree on those terms.

Anyway, the procurer I mentioned brought over more than a hundred and seventy beauties, all very carefully selected. But none of them would do. At this point, amid considerable gloom, my name happened to come up. A person from the village of Kowata was sent to Uji (where I lived in seclusion) to bring me back to the capital. Though presented at once, just as I was, I so far surpassed the woman in the painting from Edo that further search was abandoned. The details were settled exactly as I wished. I became what people call 'a separate consort'.

I was escorted all the way to the province of Musashi and established in my lord's mansion at Asakusa.[18] Night and day I enjoyed myself: I lived among flowers like those of a Chinese Mount Yoshino;[19] I summoned theatrical troupes from Sakai-chō, and spent the night laughing. Surrounded by luxury beyond my dreams, still I suffered from a woman's weakness. There was one thing I missed. . . .

However, military households have strict rules. The ladies of the inner apartments seldom even see a man, much less catch the scent of a loin-cloth. When they look at those delightful erotic pictures by Moronobu, they suddenly begin to feel rather skittish and amorous. They cannot help drawing up their heels and curling their middle fingers. But solitary pleasure does not satisfy them, since they want real love.

For the most part, the *daimyō* are extremely busy at their official duties. Sooner or later they feel compassion for the young pages who attend them closely morning and night; for their female attendants, too, they have a special sympathy, and a keen one. Their true wives never enter their minds. This, when you stop to think of it, is surely because these ladies are free from vulgar jealousy. High and low, the world over, there is nothing so frightful as a woman nagging about love.

Difficult as my position was, I aroused strong feelings in my lord. Joyfully I went to bed with him—but nothing came of it! Though still young, he depended on *jiō* pills [20] . . . and at that he never managed to finish. Such incredible bad luck! Unable to mention it to anyone, I grieved from morning till night. And meanwhile the master gradually wasted away, and began to look quite repulsive. To my surprise, people blamed *me*, saying, 'It's all because of the passion of that girl from the capital!' So the chief elders, who were ignorant about love, handled the matter according to their own judgement. I was abruptly dismissed and sent home to my parents once again.

Experience teaches that a lack of virility is sad indeed—especially for a woman!

WANTON BEAUTIES

AT the west gate of Kiyomizu Temple I heard this song, accompanied on the *samisen*:

> 'How cruel the floating world,
> Its solaces how few—
> And soon my unmourned life
> Will vanish with the dew.'

The voice, though gentle, came from a beggar-woman—the sort who would have on padded clothes in summer, or unlined ones in the cold of winter . . . and that day a fierce wind blew down from the surrounding mountains.

When I asked about her past I learned that she had been a famous *tayū* (known as 'the second Katsuragi') at the time the pleasure quarter was still in Rokujō.[21] Such is the way of the world! That very autumn, going to look at the crimson cherry leaves, I had pointed her out and laughed at her, along with the other women in my company. Yet who knows what fate will bring?

I myself suffered from the distresses of my parents. Merely because someone asked him to, my father innocently stood security for a business deal. Then the fellow disappeared. Since we had no other way to make up the lost money, I was sold to the Kambayashi tea-house in the Shimabara—for fifty *ryō*. An unexpected calling! I was already sixteen years old: a late-rising moon,[22] but, according to my master, unrivalled in the Moon Capital. He held great hopes for my future.

In general, girls begin their apprenticeship to this uncertain career in childhood. They learn the tricks of the trade without any special instruction. But although I was a late-comer, I soon picked up their manners and customs, which are quite different from those of ordinary townspeople.

A courtesan shaves her eyebrows and paints on thick black ones. Her coiffure is a full Shimada (with no underpinning); it is unobtrusively fastened by a single paper cord, folded narrow and flat; all stray hairs are regarded as loathsome and plucked

172

at once. Her kimono is made in the latest fashion, with two-and-a-half-foot sleeves—the skirt flared, not padded at the waist, the contour of the rear as smooth as possible. Her wide, unlined sash is carelessly knotted, and the undersash (for an underskirt of triple width) is tied higher than that of the ordinary woman. She wears three layers of kimono. On promenade, barefoot, she walks with an insinuatingly hesitant 'floating step'; she goes into a tea-house with a 'buoyant step'; she joins a party with a 'stealthy step'; she climbs stairs with a 'hastening step'. She never looks at her sandals as she slips them on; nor does she give way to anyone who comes towards her.

And then there is her famous 'seductive glance', with which she may turn to look at a strange man on the corner as if she finds him irresistible. Or perhaps one evening she sees a familiar guest at a tea-house entrance. After gazing at him from a distance, she nonchalantly goes over and sits down. If no one is looking she will even slip her hand into the hand of his jester, and make a point of admiring this fellow's crest, or the way his hair is done, or his smart fan—nothing of the slightest charm escapes her. 'Lady-killer!' she cries. 'Who told you you could wear your hair like that?' Tapping him playfully, she gets up and leaves.

Who can resist such wiles? The poor jester thinks he will soon make a conquest. Forgetting his own interests, he praises her to his master, and even when people gossip he takes the blame for her. Of course it is also easy (and inexpensive) to please a man by tearing up an old letter,[23] crumpling it into a ball, and flinging it at him. But simpletons would never think of that.

Yet if even a beauty in great demand excuses herself from entertaining guests on the special festival days,[24] she will be treated rather abruptly at the tea-house. She may pretend to be waiting for a gentleman, but she will find herself sitting in a dark corner, without a table, eating a meal of cold rice with plain soy-sauce over half-pickled eggplant—and glad if no one notices her. When she goes home, too, and sees the look on her mistress's face, she says 'Draw the bath-water' in a subdued voice. Her other experiences are equally unpleasant. But to neglect free-spending guests and be always idle—this is to ruin her master, as well as to put on foolish airs. Rather, a woman of pleasure who is at a drinking party, or such, should

XVIII. 'Wanton Beauties'

From the right three gentlemen come sauntering through the gay quarter, followed by an eager manservant. The procuress and one of the two girls

ahead of them look back enticingly; while, just beyond, another procuress and a little girl accompany a courtesan who seems intent on reading a letter. The courtesan sitting at the extreme left plucks the sleeve of a jester.

do no more than outwit her guests (tactfully) now and then, stand on ceremony a little, be hard to please, and talk sparingly.

A sophisticated guest is another matter, but an amateurish, self-styled rake feels panicky and doesn't know how to behave. In bed he seems utterly paralyzed, except for breathing heavily through his nose. If he says anything at all, his voice trembles. Though he'll pay the bill, he's as wretched as a man who has been seated in the place of honour at the tea ceremony[25] but has no idea what to do. Still, this sort of guest should not be considered a nuisance and given the cold shoulder. Since he has begun by trying to act like a man of the world, the courtesan herself will play hard to get—treat him all very civilly but fail to undo her sash, pretend to fall asleep, and so on. At this point most men will begin to snuggle up, and let their leg rest on you. But if you continue to keep silent, and then look over later, you will find that he's so worried he's dripping with sweat.

To judge from what is going on in the next room, the guest in there is either an old friend or a newcomer who knows how to break the ice. 'You're not as slender as I thought!' a courtesan can be heard to say. Then a rustling of the bedclothes. The man becomes more and more violent in his movements, shoving aside screens and pillows; the woman, too, with a heartfelt cry, suddenly snatches up her pillow and throws it. In the midst of the confusion there is a sharp snap, evidently a comb breaking. Overhead one hears someone murmuring 'Oh! when you do that . . .' and then the faint noise of a paper handkerchief in use. On the other side a man is being tickled out of a sound sleep. His partner tells him how sad she is that dawn will soon separate them, and so forth; still half-asleep, he begs 'Just one more! Before I have to leave!' She asks if he wants *sake*, but there is the rustle of a loosening undersash. An unexpectedly amorous nature—surely a happy gift for a courtesan!

This fellow, however, though surrounded by such obvious delight, is still too nervous to close his eyes. He wakes the girl up with one of the usual questions calculated to appeal to her kind: 'The Festival of the Ninth Moon [26] will soon be here,' he says; 'but no doubt you're already engaged for it.'

Of course that sort of thing is quite transparent. 'Whether it's the ninth moon or the first,' she replies coolly, 'a certain gentleman pays a great deal of attention to me.'

This seems to exhaust his stock of ingratiating remarks, so he regretfully gets up to leave, like everyone else. He dresses his hair negligently in the 'tea-whisk' style,[27] reties his sash, and behaves as if he had acquitted himself splendidly—all very amusing! At the bottom of his heart such a man feels deeply resentful towards the courtesan. Next time, he thinks, he will call for a different girl and entertain her lavishly as long as five or six days on end, to make tonight's 'vicious little harlot' sorry. Or perhaps he will stop visiting this quarter altogether, and begin chasing after young actors. Hastily he calls his companions, who are reluctant to see the dawn of their night of love. 'Don't overdo it!' he says. 'Let's get out of here!' He is on the point of abandoning the courtesan forever—but she has a trick to hold him!

In full view of the other guests who have come with him she smooths his rumpled side-locks and, leaning close to his ear, whispers: 'A stubborn rascal who leaves before asking me to undo my sash! How hateful!' She gives him a tap on the back, and runs out to the kitchen.

Then, since everyone has noticed, his friends ask, 'How did you manage to get on such close terms at the very first meeting?'

The man is delighted. 'She's absolutely devoted to me', he tells them. 'She really spoiled me last night—I even had her massage my shoulders, since they've been a little stiff lately! I can't understand why she fell so madly in love with me. You must have told her I have a lot of money!'

'No, no!' they flatter him. 'A courtesan would never behave that way just out of greed! You shouldn't turn your back on her.' At that point she has him nicely hooked.

When even this sort of fiasco ends up so well, no wonder a man will ruin himself for a clever girl.

It doesn't pay to give an ordinary-looking man a cool reception, with some excuse that 'Since this is your first visit . . .'. The poor fellow may be overawed by the *tayū*, fumble his approach, and, feeling thoroughly chilled, get up and leave. A girl who has her career to think of shouldn't stick to attractive men. If a gentleman is well known in the capital, never mind if he's old, or has taken Buddhist orders! Of course nothing could be more desirable than a well-born young man who showers you with presents, and who is also handsome. But what chance of getting all that good luck at once?

As for the styles that modern courtesans like to see their guests adopt: a yellow-striped kimono dyed in the 'thousand-filament' pattern; over that a short crested garment of black *habutae* silk; a sash of pale orange 'dragon-gate' cloth; a coat of reddish-brown Hachijō pongee, lined with the same material. Straw sandals, worn without socks, should be discarded after a single use.

The proper guest has a lordly ease in the reception-room. His short sword hangs slightly forward. He fans himself so that the air drifts down his sleeves. After a little while he goes out to the wash-room, where, although there is water in the stone basin, he has it changed and then calmly rinses his mouth. In order to smoke he sends a little girl to fetch the tobacco (wrapped in white Hōsho paper) which he has had a servant carry for him. He places handkerchiefs of Nobe paper by his side, casually uses one and tosses it away. Summoning an attendant courtesan,[28] he says, 'Lend me your hand a moment', and has her put it up his sleeve to scratch the moxa scars on his shoulders. At his request music-girls [29] sing and play Kaga tunes—but he pays no attention. In the middle of one of the short ballads he begins to talk to the jesters. 'Yesterday the second actor in *The Seaweed-gatherer* [30] put the Takayasu school one to shame.' After this praise he continues, for example, by saying: 'I spoke to His Excellency the Chief Councillor [31] about that old poem we mentioned the other day; he confirmed that it's by Ariwara Motokata,[32] as I thought.' Thus, beginning with two or three elegant remarks, he conducts himself suavely and with great composure. Such a man impresses a *tayū*: a certain deference to him is only natural. Since whatever he does seems so formidably clever, she stops trying to awe him, and tries to please him.

All courtesans have prestige according to the luxuries their guests will pay for. When the Edo gay quarter was at its prime a connoisseur named Sakakura was the special friend of the *tayū* Chitose. This man was extremely fond of *sake*, with which he always liked to take (salted) the 'flower-crabs' from the Mogami River in the eastern provinces. One day Sakakura had an artist of the Kanō school paint his family crest (bamboo-grass in a circle) in gold on the tiny carapaces of these crabs. The painter set his fee at one *bu* each (also in gold) . . . and Chitose was kept fully supplied with them the year round!

Again, in the capital a man about town named Ishiko was intimate with the *tayū* Nokaze,[33] and got her all sorts of rare and fashionable things before anyone else had them. Thus, Nokaze's autumn wadded-silk garment was a permissible shade of red—but dotted all over in white, the centre of each dot burned out with a taper to reveal a point of deep crimson [34] wadding! To satisfy this unique whim, three *kamme* of silver went for a single kimono.

Similarly, in Osaka a man called Nizō, who engaged the late *tayū* Dewa of the Nagasaki-ya day after day, also considerably hired, to amuse *her*, a number of lonely girls of the Kuken quarter during the slack autumn season. In her garden a cluster of blossoming *hagi* had been sprinkled, so that drops of water glistened at the tips of its leaves, though the dew of evening had not yet fallen. Deeply touched by this sight, the *tayū* murmured, 'In the shadow of these very flowers a deer lonely for his mate could find a momentary refuge.[35] How I should love to see one there alive—I wouldn't even be afraid if he had horns!'

'Nothing could be simpler', replied Nizō. And he ordered the back reception-room torn down at once. A thousand *hagi* bushes were planted, to make a field within the house; all night long he had mountaineers from Tamba drive in male and female deer—quite a herd of them. The next morning he showed it to her. Then, so they say, he had the room rebuilt exactly as it was before.

To think that a girl without the slightest virtue can enjoy luxuries beyond the reach of the aristocracy! Will not Heaven chastise her some day?

Moreover, I took money from guests I didn't like, and then refused to sleep with them. But as I went on treating men unkindly (and being thought cruel in turn), one day I found myself deserted, with nothing but time on my hands. Naturally I fell below the rank of *tayū*, and began to yearn for the good old days. You can't afford to be squeamish about men unless you are at the peak of your popularity. Once you're left alone, you're delighted to meet a clerk, a gong-beating beggar, a lame man, a man with a hare-lip—anyone at all!

When you think of it, there is no other career so miserable.

COURTESAN OF MIDDLE RANK

An extraordinary spectacle! Down the new roadway from the Shujaku Gate to the gate of the Shimabara came a man riding an Ōtsu pack-horse with two sixteen-gallon *sake*-barrels lashed to its saddle. He wore a wadded-cotton kimono, vertically striped, carried a short sword without a hilt-guard, and had on a wide bamboo-sheath hat. Holding the reins in his right hand, the whip in his left, he let the horse amble along at its own pace. Thus he made his way to the Maru-ya tea-house of Shichizaemon. The attendant who came with the horse went in first and delivered his bill of goods: 'Please be advised that this gentleman has come to the capital from Murakami, in the province of Echigo, for the purpose of meeting courtesans. Kindly entertain him in lavish style. After enjoying the pleasures of your quarter, he wants to see Osaka, too; please have one of your men take him to the Sumiyoshi-ya or the Izutsu-ya. I hope you will treat him, in every respect, exactly as you would myself.'

The person who had sent this letter was known as an influential man from Echigo, the special friend of the former *tayū* Yoshino. Few rakes spent their money so freely, these days. Impossible to forget that he had paid, single-handed, the cost of building another storey! And so, arriving with an introduction of this sort, the visitor was affably told 'Please come in'. Yet when you looked at him closely, after his horse had been led away, you could hardly take him for a pleasure-seeker.

The servants, being accustomed to the urbanity of the capital, had some misgivings about him. 'Do you wish to meet our courtesans?' they inquired.

Whereupon the rustic dandy made a sour face and said, 'Don't worry about the money!' And he threw down a leather bag, from which spilled out more than half a peck of oblong coins embossed in a paulownia-stalk design. These one-*bu* gold coins, which now seldom came into anyone's hands, he distributed in handfuls. Gratefully, since it was just as the nights were becoming cold, the servants realized they could redeem their pawned winter things.

After that, he was asked to have a cup of *sake*. 'I'm used to drinking our own local brew,' he said, 'and I can't stand any other kind. So I brought two barrels of this *sake* all the way with me, and mean to stay as long as it holds out. Don't expect me to pour a drink of it for anybody!'

'If the *sake* of the capital does not please you,' the proprietor replied, 'no doubt our courtesans will also be too delicate for your taste. What sort of women do you prefer? Let me show you our *tayū.*'

The rake laughed. 'I don't care what the bedding is like, and you can't tell what a woman's disposition'll be. So never mind *showing* me anyone—just bring on the best-looking *tayū* in the quarter!'

'But merely for your amusement', said the proprietor, and he led him out to see all the courtesans in their evening finery. Each in turn he named, pointing with a gold or silver fan. Instead of announcing her rank, he indicated a *tayū* with a gesture of his gold fan, a courtesan of second rank with his silver one. Another trick of the trade.

When I was a *tayū*, I prided myself on my superior ancestry—not that anyone knew whether you were the daughter of a Court noble or a rag-picker's child! And I was particularly vain of my good looks. I received all my guests with a bored, indifferent air, refused to see them off at cock-crow, and never so much as spoke to an unsophisticated man. Naturally this gave me a bad reputation. My guests became fewer and fewer, until at last the proprietor could bear it no longer. After consulting with all the others, he lowered my rank. From that day on I had no retinue of courtesans, I slept on two layers of bedding instead of three, even the kitchen-maid stopped bowing to me, and persons who had called me 'Mistress' now called me 'Miss'. And I was no longer seated in the place of honour. How many indignities I suffered daily!

As *tayū*, I never spent the day without being called to a tea-house. Some guests asked for engagements three weeks in advance; every day invitations came to me from four or five different places. Messengers raced back and forth from the tea-houses on my account, and wherever I went guests

XIX. 'Courtesan of Middle Rank'

Right: A rustic guest arrives at the Maru-ya (Circle House—marked by the circle on the slashed curtain at the door). His pack-horse man presents the

invaluable letter of introduction. Left: He dumps out some of his gold coins in the respectful presence of the proprietor and his wife. On the veranda is one of his *sake*-barrels.

clamoured to have me greet them or see them off. But now, attended by one little apprentice, I walked quietly along in the midst of the crowd.

Still, the Maru-ya's guest from Echigo fell in love with me at first sight. 'That's the girl!' he said.

'Only today, sir,' he was told, 'she's been reduced to the second rank.'

'I just came here to impress the folks at home, so I don't want anyone less than a *tayū*. I've seen quite a few girls, and she's the most beautiful of 'em all—if you lowered *her* rank, there must be something secretly wrong with her!'

Inevitably a rumour of that sort began to spread.

I received men I had hated the day before. Though I did my best to behave well at parties, something always upset me. For the first time, I dropped a *sake*-cup! Whatever I said or did was wrong. Even in bed I was afraid of my guests, and used every trick to please them. I dressed quickly; I became so thrifty I hated to burn incense; when the upstairs servant announced 'Your bedroom is ready', I only had to be called once or twice before hurrying up the steps. The mistress of the house would follow me to the door and ask my guest 'Have you retired, sir?' Then, turning to leave, she would snap 'Go to bed!' at me. On her way downstairs she would scold the maid: 'Put out the candles in there and give them an oil lamp. And I wonder what idiot took *them* the raised-lacquer boxes of food I ordered for the large room!' Of course she knew we could hear every word, but that didn't disturb her a bit. This was only one of many changes in my treatment since I lost prestige as a courtesan.

There were other such remarks too. Paying no attention, I would drop off to sleep—till my guest wakened me. After he had had his fill of love-making he might inquire sympathetically about my parents. And I would tell him everything, purely out of greed. Naturally we opened our hearts to each other. I would even bring up the matter of my New Year's outfit. If he promised to pay for most of it, it made me so happy I'd treat him as an intimate friend—go all the way to the main gate at parting, and wait there till he was out of sight. Then I would send a messenger after him, with an elaborate letter.

When I was a *tayū* I didn't even write to regular guests who had called on me six or seven times. Noticing this, my mistress and my attendants would urge 'Do write a letter to Mr. So-and-so!' As soon as they thought I was in an especially good humour they mixed fresh ink on the ink-stone and brought me thick Hōsho paper. I scribbled down a few hackneyed phrases, had someone fold and seal it, then addressed it and tossed it aside. And the reply would come by way of one of my attendants: 'I am deeply grateful for your letter, and hope that you will continue to think as kindly of me . . .' and so on. There might even be a present of three gold *ōban*,[36] delivered through my mistress.

At that time, money meant nothing to me. I didn't hesitate to give away gold and silver, for which others were so greedy; of course a *tayū* thinks no more of such coins than a gambler does of copper ones. But now that I was out of money I had to swallow my pride and ask for it—which is not to say I got it!

As a rule, men spend more on courtesans than they can afford. Those who have over five hundred *kamme* of silver at their disposal are perhaps eligible to meet a *tayū*. Men with two hundred *kamme* or more are able to stand the strain of a second-rank courtesan; with fifty *kamme* they can have a girl of the third rank. Those who are merely living on their capital, without putting it to work in a business, shouldn't dream of visiting the pleasure quarter. What actually happens, these days, is that men whose money won't last half a year go out on reckless sprees, ruin themselves by borrowing at twenty or thirty per cent interest, and cause their masters and relatives a great deal of trouble. Once you know you have something like that to look forward to, how can you possibly enjoy yourself?

In this floating world anything can happen. While I was a second-rank courtesan, I had three guests I thought I could count on. One was an Osaka man, who went bankrupt trying to corner betel-nut; another put a lot of money into the theatre, and lost it; the third failed in a mining venture. Within three weeks all three were ruined. Nothing more was heard of them, and I suddenly found myself quite alone. Then, too, about the time when the frosts came I began to be troubled with little swellings, the size of millet-seeds, under my ears. And they left ugly blemishes. To make matters worse, I caught influenza, and my black hair thinned out.

Men turned their backs on me more than ever. Resentfully, I turned my own back on my mirror.

IN THE LOWER RANKS OF THE
GAY QUARTER

SINCE even the lowest townsman carries a short sword the world is spared many arguments and quarrels.[37] If samurai were the only ones allowed to carry swords, a little man would always be at the mercy of a big, strong fellow. With a single blade to keep other men at a distance you can walk alone on the darkest night. Now a courtesan likes dashing men. So she is delighted to have someone pick a fight over her, and is even ready to sacrifice her own life. 'I too am a courtesan!' I said; and I was firmly resolved, day in and day out, to lay down my life for honour on the very spot. But even though I had sunk so low, I could hardly do this without the co-operation of a gentleman.

Much as the fall from *tayū* had disturbed me, I now slipped still another rank. Strangely enough, my disposition changed too, and I looked at everything from the point of view of a third-rank courtesan.

Called for 'somebody new', I was so glad to have a customer I didn't ask anyone to see what he looked like. I hurried to him at once, fearful that if he changed his mind I'd have the whole day to myself. Even so, a tea-house servant yelled out, for my benefit: 'Get a third-rate prostitute who'll come when she's called. A cheap whore can't afford to waste time dressing up— she'll be lucky to get her eighteen *momme*!' Not only was *this* painful, but the mistress of the house, pretending she didn't see me, refused to give me a word of greeting.

To cover my embarrassment I went out to the kitchen, where I happened to find the proprietor of a tea-shop near the Tamba Gate. 'Go on upstairs', he said; and as he pointed with one hand, he tickled me with the other, behind. A little annoyed at this, I went to the reception-room. The wealthy rakes were attended by *tayū*, in equal number, and their companions by girls of the second rank. Besides these, there were four or five young men to amuse the party. I was called over to join them, without any special partner, and was given the lowest seat in the room. A *sake*-cup came to me (after it had made the rounds), but no one poured a drop into it. In fact, no one paid any attention whatever to me. So I passed the cup to a music-girl beside me, and waited impatiently for nightfall.

When I went to my single-layer bed, it was with a rather too neat young fellow, who looked exactly like a neighbourhood barber. At best, he may have known his way around the brothels of Koppori-chō or Uehakken: his bed manners were ludicrous. He took off his sash, arranged paper handkerchiefs within reach, and then, doubtless to impress me, drew the lamp nearer the pillow and emptied his purse of one *bu* in gold and some thirty *momme* in silver coins, which he counted over and over. An impossible person! When he tried to begin a conversation, I told him I had a sudden pain in my stomach—and turned over to go to sleep. Talking me out of it obviously didn't occur to him. All he said was 'I have the best medicine for that here in my hand.' And he spent the whole night applying it! Finally, out of pity, I rolled over towards him, intending to put my arms around him and make love with a good grace.

Just then we were rudely aroused by the voice of one of the wealthy guests: 'It'll soon be daylight! You go home first—someone may be waiting to have his hair done.' When I heard this my mood changed again. Realizing I'd guessed right about his trade, and so all the more fearful of ruining my reputation, I promptly jumped out of bed and left him.

While serving in the higher ranks I felt that this life, bad as it was, was not so bad after all. But now I began to realize how miserable it could be. I didn't even meet second-rate guests, and I hated the vulgar kind. Once by some rare chance I happened to meet a sophisticated man, but he was blunt enough with me. His first words in the bedroom were 'Take off your sash'.

'Don't be in such a hurry!' I answered, a little sarcastically. 'I wonder how you waited nine months in your mother's womb. . . .'

'That kind of waiting can begin now', he interrupted. 'Since the age of the gods there's been trouble with these reluctant whores.' And he went on as hastily as ever. When I objected

XX. 'In the Lower Ranks of the Gay Quarter'

Right: A boorish guest counts his money in the lamplight, but without

creating the desired impression. Left: A more pleasant tête-à-tête, as the attendant leaves.

again, his arrogant expression plainly said: 'Nothing could be simpler—I'll get rid of her and try another girl!'

Much as I feared him, I was more afraid of losing his business. So, knowing he was a man about town, I quickly put on a sugary tone of voice and said, 'I can't imagine how you'll explain it when your favourite courtesan learns you condescended to amuse yourself with *me*!' . . . and so on. This was the usual last bit of flattery among girls of the third rank.

If I told you everything that happened to me as a fourth-rank girl (the level to which I now sank), it would be an endless story—and a dull one. Besides, I used the same wiles and the same old hackneyed bed-talk on all my guests. Still, three *momme* wasn't a bad fee. When I had a guest, I came into the room in a leisurely way, followed by an apprentice-courtesan dressed in cotton. She would prepare the bedding, which was of medium-grade red silk, place attractively folded paper handkerchiefs close at hand, turn down the oil-lamp and put it aside, and arrange the two wooden pillows. Then, after saying 'Please make yourself at home', she would leave through a little side-door.

Even prostitutes of my low rank didn't always have excessively vulgar guests. Some were men who had spent more than they could afford, and now slunk past certain tea-house gates only after dark; others were the clerks of rich shopkeepers; still others belonged to the lower orders of the samurai class.

After lying in bed for a while without undoing my sash, I would clap hands to call my little servant, and say to her, tenderly, 'Please take my kimono, shabby as it is, and put it over the foot of the bed.' Then I would notice his fan. 'Is it possible', I might ask, for example, 'that that figure of a nobleman covering his head with his sleeve alludes to the poem about "a snowy evening at the Sano ferry"?'[38]

This would give him an excuse to nestle close to me. 'Indeed, your own skin is as white as "the snow shaken off my sleeves". Suppose I caress it a bit. . . .' At which point we began our love-making.

A guest who didn't ask the girl's name till he took his leave was clearly a man of distinction. But there is a trick to hold men of this sort. At parting, as you see him off a little way, you

remark, 'Now I suppose it's time to visit your favourite courtesan.' Any man will show off by coming back again to start a
lovers' quarrel. Then he is in your clutches.

Or, if I met a shop-assistant, I said something like, 'You
worry me by the way you go out in the streets alone at night,
without taking a servant along.' None of them ever replied, 'I
don't have any servants.' And this flattery had a special purpose: later, when we were sufficiently intimate for me to
request a large box [39] of clothing, they could hardly say, 'But I
have no one to carry it!'

At the level of a two-*momme* girl, I myself had to turn down
the lamp and spread paper on the pillows. I'd sing a familiar
part of one of Kadayū's ballads, then break off and say, 'I
wonder who you visit regularly. You must find it tiresome
being in a place like this, even for a little while. Which tea-
house do you go to?' Of course these were the usual stale
compliments.

At the one-*momme* fee, I would sing some new popular song
as I drew a straw sleeping-mat from behind a folding screen . . .
and slipped my sash off the very first thing. Regardless of my
guest's feelings, I followed the house rule by stripping off my
clothes, undergarments and all, and tucking them out of sight.
To a guest who was already in a hurry I would say, 'It still
seems like early evening, but wasn't that the midnight bell?
How far do you have to go?' As soon as we finished I called my
mistress and said quickly, 'Please bring us tea in a pair of
Temmoku bowls.' Coming from me, that sounded ridiculous!

At half a *momme*, I closed the door myself, spread a narrow
Toshima-mat with one hand, pushed the tobacco-tray into
place with my foot, and pulled my guest down to me. 'A gentleman with a worn-out loin-cloth, but a silk one!' I would exclaim. 'You're obviously used to luxury—let me see if I can
guess what you do. Since you're free on a moon-lit night when
there's no wind, you're a night-watchman, aren't you?'

'No,' he might answer, 'I'm a big broker in the seaweed-
jelly [40] trade.'

'Don't talk nonsense!' I would say. 'You'd be out peddling
your jelly on a nice warm night like this. And tonight's the
summer festival at the Kōzu Temple—you'd make eighty *mon*
at the very least!'

Whatever trade was mentioned, I thought of something appropriately clever.

When I lost *that* rank, I was sold to the Shimmachi quarter.[41] During my two years of cheap prostitution there I had all sorts of experiences. At last my thirteen-year term of service ended.[42] Since no one had taken *me*, I took a Yodo River boat and went back home again.[43]

There follows a Boccaccian episode in which Saikaku's heroine (like Kiseki's 'Wayward Wife') adopts masculine dress and hair style, in order to visit Buddhist monasteries. At one she becomes an intimate friend of the abbot, and contracts to remain for three years. Her health declines, but she grows accustomed to this new life. 'Even the smoke of burning corpses didn't bother my nose, since I was happy to think that the higher the mortality the better for our temple.' [44] *Then one autumn night during her first year she is visited by the resentful phantom of her predecessor, who threatens to bite her. The next day she tells the abbot she is pregnant, and he advises her to leave at once. But she must promise to come back. She agrees, knowing that the monks will scarcely take legal action against her. We next find her living decorously alone in Kyoto.*

LADY ETIQUETTE-TEACHER AND
LETTER-WRITER

'THE irises you sent me are exquisite: I gaze at them endlessly with the greatest pleasure.'

In Kyoto there are 'lady letter-writers' who make a living with this sort of thing! After serving at Court, where they learn the proper rules of upper-class etiquette for every occasion, they can easily set themselves up as teachers. And many a prosperous townsman sends his young daughter to such a woman, saying 'Follow her example!'

Years ago I, too, had been in the service of a Court lady, and because of that connexion I was able to establish a writing-school for girls. Delighted to live in my own house at last, I stuck the notice 'Instruction in Calligraphy for Ladies' on my gate-post, put my one small room in order, and hired a maid-servant fresh from the country. Taking charge of other people's daughters was no easy matter, it seemed to me. Day after day, without fail, I corrected papers and taught the essentials of feminine good manners. I even behaved myself—no more loose thoughts for me!

Then an ardent young man asked me to write love-letters for him. Since my experience at love was thoroughly professional, I had no trouble turning out a seductive letter. Whether my correspondent appeared to be an innocent young girl or a shrewd, seasoned woman of the floating world, I knew just the trick for her . . . one she was sure to find irresistible.

There is no more convenient way to express affection than by letter. With a writing-brush, you can even convey your thoughts to someone who lives far away. Of course a deceitful letter, however long and elaborate, is so revolting one doesn't hesitate to destroy it. But the traces of a sincere brush leave an indelible impression: you feel that you are in the very presence of the writer.

Now among the numerous gentlemen I met during my years in the pleasure quarter there was one I particularly loved. In

XXI. 'Lady Etiquette-teacher and Letter-writer'

Three young girls (one carrying a box of writing materials and a copy-book) leave to the right. A sign on the door-post reads: 'Instruction in Calligraphy for Ladies.' At the left the heroine is writing a love-letter for a

young man, as her servant brings tea. Brushes and ink-stone lie in the lacquer box before her; a rather showy kimono with a water-wheel pattern hangs from the clothes-rack next to the folding screen.

his arms I forgot all about being a prostitute; I trusted him completely and opened my heart to him. Though the man didn't forsake me, he found at last, as our love grew, that he could no longer afford to visit me. I was sorry, and secretly wrote to him every day. Apparently my letters made him feel as if we were together again. After reading them over and over, he took them to bed with him. Then, dozing off with his arms around them, he would dream that these letters changed into my own image. And he would talk to me the whole night through—to the alarm of others who were lying near him! I heard all this later, after he was back on his feet and able to visit me as before. Day by day, my thoughts had been communicated to him exactly.

And that was only natural. If you concentrate when you write a letter, put your whole mind to it and forget everything else, your thoughts will certainly not go astray.

So I poured all my passion into writing on behalf of young men. 'When you have *me* do your love-letters,' I assured them, 'you're likely to get just what you want—no matter how hard-hearted she is.' Before I knew it, my letters even began to convince myself! I fell in love with a customer.

One day, as I sat beside him, brush in hand, I lapsed into a long, pensive silence. Then I spoke out shamelessly. 'This woman keeps you in suspense by cruelly refusing to give in to you. She's utterly inhuman. Rather than go on wasting your time, why not take me instead? We can get together on this. Leave my looks out of the question—I'm good-natured, and willing to make love with you right away. Can you do any better for the present?'

This startled him. He was silent a moment, and seemed to be thinking, 'Since I don't know what lies ahead I might as well take a short-cut.' Evidently he noticed my curly hair, my small mouth, and the way my big toes curved back.[45] 'I'll be frank', he said. 'Even if *I* had approached *you*, I wouldn't dream of paying for love. You won't get a single sash out of me. Later, after we become more intimate, perhaps you'll ask if I know a good place to buy cloth, or something of the sort. But I can't absolutely guarantee you so much as a bolt of ordinary silk or a few yards of red silk. I tell you this now, so there'll be no misunderstanding.'

He was entirely *too* frank, for a man who wanted to have his way with me! Ashamed and spiteful, I told myself there'd be no drought of men in this vast capital. Perhaps someone else. . . .

Just at that moment the early summer rains began to fall, very softly, and a wood-sparrow flew into the room and put out our light. Taking advantage of the darkness, the fellow clutched me. Soon he was breathing heavily, and the little Sugiwara paper-handkerchiefs near our pillow came into use. 'You'll do till you're a hundred',[46] he said, patting my hip gently.

'Don't be ridiculous!' I thought. 'Would I let a foolhardy wretch like you live to ninety-nine? I hate what you said just now, and within a year I'll make you walk with a stick, give you a shrivelled chin, and drive you out of this floating world!'

I began to frolic with him night and day. When he weakened, I fed him mud-fish soup, eggs, and yams. As might have been expected, he gradually withered away.

It was pitiful! The next spring, when everyone had changed to light kimono, he went on wearing layers of thickly padded clothes. One doctor after another gave him up. His beard was shaggy, his nails long. He listened with his hand cupped behind his ear—and if there was any talk about good-looking women, he turned away reproachfully.

MAIDSERVANT OF A TOWNSMAN

THAT year the season of midsummer heat lasted nineteen days,[47] which everyone thought unbearable. But suddenly the futile chatter about 'a place without summer or sweat', and so on, was interrupted by the noisy gongs and cymbals of a funeral procession. There seemed to be no heir, and the relatives attending the coffin were not exactly sunk in grief. The neighbours who followed were wearing ceremonial dress, out of a sense of duty: prayer-beads in hand, they discussed credit-suits, rice-speculation, or the great Flying Goblin hoax.[48] After them came the young men, who chatted about the bill of fare at various tea-houses and made private plans to stop at a pleasure quarter near the cemetery. At last, straggling far behind, followed a group of people who looked like tenants. One would be dressed in a two-piece combination of thin hemp and lined winter cloth; another, odder still, would be in formal footwear but without a sword, or would have on a short padded coat over a striped summer kimono of home-woven hemp. In a hubbub of loud voices they talked about such things as whale-oil lamps (were they good or bad?) [49] and fans decorated with picture-puzzles.

Really, they were all a little *too* casual! No one could overhear such talk without thinking it shameful.

A man who recognized most of these people said they belonged to the neighbourhood at Gokō-machi, above the Seigan Temple.[50] So the funeral must have been for the proprietor of the Tachibana-ya, a shop on the west side of the street. His wife, you see, was very beautiful—amusing to think how many men had gone there, merely to look at her, and bought more screen-paper than they could possibly use.

As Gion Jinta said, 'You'll spend the rest of your life looking at the woman you marry—but if she's too good-looking you probably won't enjoy it.' That may sound like a typical matchmaker's warning. Still, a wife's beauty brings nothing but worry to her husband. When you only want someone to stay home and

198

look after the house, there's no need to be so particular. And it's a matter of ordinary experience that, with feminine as well as scenic beauties, the same old view will inevitably begin to bore you.

One year I went to Matsushima.[51] At first I clapped my hands in delight, and thought, 'If I could show this to all the poets!' But as I gazed, day in and day out, the thousand little islands began to seem rather dreary. The noise of the much-poeticized 'surf at Sue-no-matsuyama' grated on my ears; the 'cherry blossoms at Shiogama' were scattered before I cared to look at them. I slept too late for the 'snowy dawns at Mount Kinka', and saw nothing special in the 'moonlit evenings at Nagane and Oshima'. Finally I gathered black and white stones along the inlet and killed the time playing fox and geese with children.

Take another example. When a man who is used to Osaka goes to the capital he marvels at the beauty of Higashiyama—just as a Kyoto man thinks the sea-coast is wonderful, simply because he seldom visits it. In the same way, it is all very well so long as a man's wife keeps up her appearance for her husband. Later, though, she does her hair hastily, strips to the waist and lets him see the mole on her side, and one day, ambling more carelessly than usual, reveals that her left foot is a bit longer than her right. One by one, her defects appear. Then she has a baby, and the disenchantment is complete.

This may suggest that men shouldn't have wives, but I've seen enough of the world to know they can't do without them. Once I went sightseeing deep into the Yoshino mountains. There weren't even any cherry blossoms, not to mention real live human beings—except for ascetics.[52] As I picked my way along the edge of a lonely cliff I came to a man living in a little sloped-roof hut. It looked as if there were no amusements besides listening to the wind in the cedars by day and watching the flame of a pine-torch by night. 'You could be living in the capital', I told him. 'How can you stand it here, of all places?'

The yokel grinned. 'It's not so bad', he said. 'I've got my old woman to take my mind off it.'

Sure enough! There's only one pleasure you really can't get along without.

A woman doesn't enjoy living alone, either. So I dropped my calligraphy pupils and hired myself out as a personal maid, in the service of a cloth merchant whose shop was called the Daimonji-ya. People used to prefer maidservants in their early teens; now, though, for reasons of economy, they take girls in the late teens and early twenties. These, they say, have not only the looks to go out in attendance on a palanquin but the strength to handle bedding at home.

Much as I hated tying my sash at the back,[53] I changed my style completely. Now I wore a modestly cut deep-orange kimono in a zigzag pattern of medium size; I did my hair in a plain 'middle Shimada', tied with a cheap paper cord. No one could have been more innocent.

'See how the snow drifts down!' I said to the old woman who ran the house. 'What do you suppose it's made of?'

'A fine question at your age! You've certainly led a sheltered life.'

After that, as far as she was concerned, I could get away with anything.

And I blushed violently if a man happened to take my hand, jumped if he brushed my sleeve, made sure to scream if he told a spicy story, no matter how delightful. Finally people gave me a new name: Shy Monkey. They compared my beauty to the blossoms of a flowering tree, and my shyness to a wild monkey in the tree-top. My artless manner was a complete success.

How strange that people can be so stupid! Though it was my secret shame to have had eight abortions, I found that the hardest thing to bear, as a close personal attendant, was listening night after night to the frolics of my mistress—and especially of my master. He was a lustful man, and made no attempt to hide it. Boisterously he scattered screens and pillows in his love-making, till the very doors and windows rattled. At last it was too much for me. I got up to relieve myself, quite unnecessarily, and went to see what I could find in the kitchen. Unfortunately there wasn't a scrap of man.

But in a corner of the pantry I found an old fellow lying curled up alone—a trusted servant, keeping watch over the fish-cupboard. Thinking that I would at least be reminded of better times, I stepped squarely in the middle of his ribs.

'Praise Amida! Praise Amida!' he cried. 'Even with the light burning, they still bother an old man!'

'I stepped on you by accident', I said. 'But if you can't forgive me, do whatever you like—this foot is to blame!' And I thrust it inside the old fellow's night-clothes.

'Hey!' He shrank back in alarm, and began to babble 'Praise Kannon! Deliver me from evil!'

I saw that my advances were getting nowhere, so I slapped his face and went back, considerably disturbed, to my own bed. I could hardly wait for dawn.

Finally it came. And since it was the morning of the twenty-eighth,[54] I'd been told to begin cleaning the household Buddhist shrine, among other things, before the stars faded from the sky. My mistress, still dog-tired from the night before, didn't get up. But my master was a vigorous man. He broke the ice in the water-basin, washed his face, and put on a ceremonial coat [55] over his night-kimono. Then, sacred book in hand, he asked me, 'Aren't the offerings ready yet?'

I went very close to him. 'Does your scripture explain the art of love?' I inquired.

The master was too shocked to answer.

With a smile, I added, 'Nobody dislikes *that* doctrine!' Putting on a sultry manner, I nonchalantly began to take off my sash.

The master couldn't bear it. Ceremonial coat and all, he behaved most improperly; his violent gestures rocked the image of the Buddha and knocked over the tortoise-shaped candlestick. I made him forget all about Buddhism.

After that I had him as a secret lover. Naturally I became so impudent that I paid no attention to my mistress's orders. At last I schemed to have her divorced, which was dreadful even for me!

I had a certain hermit-priest put a curse on her, but it didn't work. I myself burned with anger. As this feeling grew more intense, I blackened my teeth, stuck thin-skinned bamboo toothpicks in my mouth, and uttered curses of my own. But even these didn't have the slightest effect on her. Instead, I was the one who suffered. Before I knew it, I had let the cat out of the bag—I told the whole shameful story of deceit, which gave my master a scandalous reputation. Years of misconduct were revealed all at once. It was exactly the sort of thing any respectable person ought to be discreet about!

Then I went crazy: one day I would show my face at the

XXII. 'Maidservant of a Townsman'

Right: In the pantry. The heroine (dressed for bed) excuses herself for stepping on the old man who was asleep near the fish-cupboard. Left: She

distracts her master from his sacred books. In the background is a Buddhist altar with incense-burner, tortoise-shaped candlestick, etc. Her mistress sleeps soundly in the next room.

Gojō Bridge; the day before, my gaunt figure would have been seen in Murasakino. Wandering as if in a dream, I brought the mad dance of Komachi to life. 'Oh, how I want a man!' I chanted, and every note I sang was about love.[56]

'That's the end of the passionate maidservant', people said.

On I danced, fluttering my fan,[57] till I reached an Inari shrine gate before a deep, cool grove of cedars. Finally aware that I was stark naked, I came to my senses. My evil thoughts were dispelled. Alas! I knew my vile curses had brought swift retribution. I repented and went home.

There is nothing more fragile than a woman. It's a cruel world!

Again, after serving briefly as attendant to the jealous wife of a feudal lord in Edo, she goes back to Osaka. There she joins a group of 'singing nuns'— prostitutes, in fact—who row out to solicit travellers sleeping on ship-board in the harbour. These women were paid only three momme. *But at that, she says, she soon managed to empty the purses of three men.*

The next episode begins with her complaint (in part repeated by Kiseki) that modern women spend far too much time on their appearance. 'Still,' she observes, 'it's better to be good-looking, if you have the choice!' [58] *Unfortunately, the mistress whom she now goes to serve as hair-dresser is beautiful only with the aid of secret hair-pieces, unknown even to her husband. This lady, too, is jealous, and treats her badly. In return Saikaku's narrator trains a cat to paw at her coiffure, and thus one night to expose her mistress's defect. Then it is easy enough to seduce the husband.*

After an interval as professional bridesmaid for extravagant Osaka families, she settles down to a quiet life as a seamstress. She gives up all thought of men—until one day, happening to look at the lining of a young gentleman's silk undergarment, she sees an extremely life-like erotic picture. Soon she is back at her old trade, which she now plies from house to house on the pretext of doing needlework.

Later, on a holiday during another term of domestic service in Edo, she has a frustrating, low-comedy adventure with an old man who has fallen hopelessly in love with her. And her next bit of reminiscence is in the same ribald vein. Hired to take care of a rich shopkeeper now in Buddhist retirement, she decides to get a secret lover, become pregnant, and, by presenting her master with the child, claim a fat inheritance. But this scheme fails. It turns out that the 'old master' is really a woman—who wants to anticipate being born as a man in the next life! [59]

RUINED BY LOVE IN ISHIGAKI [60]

E VERY now and then I got sick of selling my love, but when
I was hard up I went back to the same old line. I learned
the tricks used by the girls at the Kurumi-ya, and, sinking to
their level, became a Kyoto tea-house girl myself. Much as I
disliked wearing long, open-cut sleeves [61] again, I had the
delicately built woman's advantage of being able to look
younger than my age. Whether in China or Japan, men always
prefer their women to be young. That is why Su Tung-p'o
wrote, 'Twenty-eight-year-old beauties apply their make-up
skilfully.' And, truly, 'a single pair of jade arms will pillow a
thousand men' [62]—no wonder we're kept busy in bed, day and
night! However, it's interesting work, for a woman who enjoys
it.

Sometimes I had clerks and artisans, some es even priests,
or actors. Still, though I frisked with all sorts of guests, I wasn't
particularly happy. When I thought how innumerable were
my intimate friendships, and how brief, it seemed to me that my
feelings towards a man—no matter if I liked him or disliked
him—were those you might have towards a fellow ssenger
on a ferry-boat before it reached the opposite bank. I talked
with the men I found attractive, but even then it wasn't heart-
to-heart talk. As for the others, I turned my head away, let my
thoughts wander, and counted the cross-pieces in the ceiling
as I waited for them to get it over with. Thus I lived, drifting
down the muddy stream of the floating world.

While I was in Ishigaki I had a splendid, fair-complexioned
guest, a man who took his pleasure secretly but in elegant style.
The rich scent of his glossy skin, rubbed sleek with oil of aloes-
wood! Later I asked a well-informed person who it might have
been. When I heard he was 'one of the wealthiest rakes in the
capital', I couldn't help feeling ashamed. From time to time
other refined gentlemen condescended to visit me. I suppose
they were all great personages of some sort.

The so-called tea-houses of this quarter had as many as seven
or eight girls each, and their customers were fashionably

dressed. Since I had picked up the manners of the Shimabara, and was not unskilful at handling a *sake*-cup, even prominent uptown gentlemen called me 'a clever little rascal'. I was trained by Gansai; [63] I learned how to amuse guests from Kagura; Ranshu's way of presenting a *sake*-cup and Ōmu's witty story-telling came to me very easily. . . . I really knew this business! But then, having gradually lost my looks again, I lost my job.

How the view changes as you drift downstream! I next went to Gion and Yasaka, where I was kept very busy. I even had to be enticing through a bamboo-blind, and call 'Won't you please come in here?' So degrading!

Our guests were pleasure-bent fellows who would go down the hill from Kiyomizu Temple, comparing girls all along the way, then uphill again, down and up, six or seven times, till they were quite exhausted. One such pair of footsore guests might be a silversmith and a roof-thatcher. Agreeing on a day when the former needed to relax and the latter expected rain, they had set out—each with the necessary two *momme*. For them it was a once-in-a-lifetime outing, as rare as a flowering stone (or one of their tips).

Two prostitutes might entertain five guests, who drew lots for their turns as soon as they sat down. They also gobbled up the salted-clams before the *sake* arrived, threw *kaya*-nut shells in the tobacco tray instead of the receptacle close at hand, wet their combs in the water of a flower-vase, and, when they were passed the *sake*-cup, carefully returned it, in the way one does at the New Year.

During a long evening with boors of this sort I suddenly found myself in the middle of a yawn. And then, just as I thought I really couldn't bear another moment, I heard the old woman receive new guests. 'Just wait here a few minutes', she said, showing them into the next room. 'The gentlemen in there will be leaving presently.'

Still another party sat below, near the tea-kettle. 'Mistress!' they called. 'You're doing well tonight!'

'Come along!' she answered. 'You'll find you don't need to stand on ceremony with these gentlemen.' And she led them upstairs too.

At this point two or three men looked in through the door.

'We'll stop by on our way back from Ryōzen', they told her, and went on. Indeed, pleasure can keep you busy!

Meanwhile, I dragged a cheap print screen over to hide one corner of the room, arranged two wooden pillows behind it, and, still standing, took off my sash and threw it aside. Chanting a snatch of ballad about 'a painful duty', I pulled my partner down by his ear and told him, rather affectedly, 'Do wash a bit around there—it won't cost you anything. Come a little closer. Oh, how awful! Your hands and feet are like ice!' And I wriggled my body violently.

When that man got up and left, there was someone else. But almost before I finished saying 'Come on, whoever you are!' I was half asleep, and snoring. Then I was tickled awake again, and let this man do as he pleased with me. Afterwards, no sooner had I washed than I was hustled out to another waiting guest.

And when I finished him off, I was summoned to a second-floor party by an impatient burst of clapping. Here, the guests were extremely angry. 'This *sake* isn't fit to drink,' one of them said, 'but isn't *anybody* coming to serve it to us? Or do you want us to go home? We're spending the same kind of money, yet you have the nerve to treat us like poison! Even if we went to all the hundred-and-nineteen tea-houses around here, I'll bet we wouldn't find another one where you get nothing but Chinese jelly-fish and this wretched sort of clam soup with your *sake*! In all our lives we've never passed bad money, and we've never borrowed umbrellas without returning them. If you're judging us by the cut of our collars, we resent it. Our kimono are wadded-cotton ones all right, but you don't see any patches on 'em!' And he flaunted his smart eight-and-a-half-inch sleeve-ends in my face.

While I was doing my best to soothe their feelings, a voice shouted, 'Hey, pie-face! Your underskirt fell off the clothes-line!'

Then a scream. 'The cat's got the fish-cakes I was just going to put out!'

Now the other back-room guests were going home, and they left a packet of money as they went. It was nimbly snatched up and weighed, roughly, in the hand; then, even before the guests were out of sight, it was put on the scales, taken to be

XXIII. 'Ruined by Love in Ishigaki'

A busy tea-house, where two footsore fellows sit near a tobacco-tray waiting their turn to go inside. Upstairs, a man who wants *sake* is being mollified.

At the lower right is the 'stone wall' (*ishigaki*) protecting the river embankment.

seen next door, and so on. All this was busier than a one-man show!

Granted that it's a way to make a living, is there any other career so shameful, or so demanding? Of course my pay gradually went up—from three to five hundred, even to eight hundred *momme*. But each of us had to get her entire wardrobe at her own expense. Since we all paid for whatever we needed, including sashes and undersashes, underwear, paper handkerchiefs, ornamental combs, down to our very hair-oil and our last toothpick, money didn't stick to our hands. Not only that: whether I had to send money home, or, on a slack evening, pay my share of the cost of dinner, there was a steady drain on my purse. I couldn't possibly save enough to get married, so I made a constant companion of my *sake* bottle. I hadn't the faintest idea what would become of me.

Then my looks faded still more and I was hired out for a month to a very busy house, while its young mistress was ill. Under all my thick make-up I was only skin and bones—and skin like goose-flesh at that. One man who knew how it felt said, for everyone to hear, 'The woman is no bargain even if *she* pays *you*.' That really hurt. Racking my brains for some other way to make a living, I nursed a grudge against the God of Passion.

Gradually I became a rather wilted blossom. Still, there are worms who prefer nettles. I had an extraordinary stroke of luck: a certain gentleman took a fancy to me, old as I was, fell head over heels in love, and began to buy me kimono of sheer black Indian silk. What's more, he didn't throw me over. Instead, he took me away from all this and set me up as his regular mistress in a separate establishment in Monzen-chō.

The gentleman in question was one of the most polished and notorious rakes of all Kyoto. Even now he is on intimate terms with the great *tayū* Takahashi, who massages his shoulders and does anything else he likes. Naturally I was delighted to form a connexion with a man of this sort . . . but what was it about me that fascinated him? Especially in Kyoto, where women are so plentiful, a man who took *me* off the shelf must have been a poor judge of quality. I was like a treasured painting or tea-caddy which is actually an expensive fake.

A bought woman should be picked out with the greatest care!

Of course her good fortune does not last. Saikaku's heroine next finds work as a bath girl—promiscuous, badly paid work, by her old standards. Then, after a short illness, she marries a fan-maker who hopes she will lure customers into his shop. This she does (he pretends not to notice when anyone pats her), and business prospers. Indeed, one young man begins to come every day, which disturbs even her indulgent husband. She leaves home, tries to find her steady customer (but cannot), and has to shift for herself once again. Among her various jobs is one as concubine to a retired but unexpectedly vigorous old gentleman. 'When I told that story to a young fellow who takes jiō pills, he gritted his teeth in vexation!' [64]

After that she finds a position (no better than usual) entertaining customers for Osaka wholesale merchants. Though soon as slatternly as the other girls, she remains much cleverer. Thanks to her persuasiveness a man from Akita signs a love pledge with her, and then, when he wants to go home to the provinces, pays up handsomely.

Her next place is at a shabby, disreputable house, where she must give the proprietor half of what little money she gets from the men who come there. Now she is among real whores: vulgar, sweating creatures who make no pretence of having refined manners or fashionable small talk. And in the following episode she displays her skills (and, alas, her wrinkles) to the boorish guests of several provincial inns. Failing even at this, she becomes a pedlar of rouge and needles in a small harbour-town. Yet she often goes aboard ship and does business without opening her pack of wares.

Later, she takes work as a procuress, but finds it unsuited to her temperament. Worse yet, she begins to lose her zest for the floating world. At sixty-five, people say she looks in her forties, which seems rather cold comfort. One night she has a horrible vision of her ninety-odd children who have died by abortion; their tears and accusations make her regret her past. But dawn comes, and she feels that life, bitter as it is, would be hard to give up. She falls in with a group of thickly painted and powdered harridans, and hears about the young men they have sold themselves to, very cheaply, under cover of darkness. They observe that beauty is unnecessary, even wasteful, in their line of work; one old hag, who would be on the streets herself if she could walk, urges her to join them—she'll do on a dark night! She agrees, and becomes one of these miserable street-walkers! Made up in their fashion and dressed in a similar rented outfit (on rainy nights she rents an umbrella at a fee larger than her own), [65] *she looks exactly like them.*

Thus, till dawn, she walks back and forth across the frosty bridges. . . .

Nowadays men are getting too clever. They put more thought into a little thing like this that a wealthy rake would into choosing a top-rank courtesan. They're so critical they wait for someone with a lantern to come by, or else take you into the lamplight from a watchman's box. Times have certainly changed. Men won't lay hands on an ugly woman, or an old one—and you don't find a blind man in a thousand any more!

Finally I counted eight bells, and then seven,[66] echoing in the dawn sky; and I heard the bustle of pack-horse men setting out, and of blacksmiths and beancurd-dealers opening their shops. Since I'd walked the streets all that time, I began to wonder if there wasn't something wrong with my style. Not a single man had spoken to me. 'This is the end of my career in the floating world', I thought. And I gave up my last shred of hope.[67]

THE BUDDHA'S FIVE HUNDRED
DISCIPLES—ALL VERY FAMILIAR!

THE mountain forests are asleep and the cherry branches are buried in snow tonight . . . but soon they will awaken with the spring dawn. Only man has nothing pleasant to look forward to as he grows old. In my own case, my past having been what it was, I couldn't even look backward for consolation. 'At least,' I thought, 'my hopes for the next world are sincere enough!' And so once again I returned to the capital, this time for the laudable purpose of visiting 'paradise on earth'—the Great Cloud Temple.

Just then there happened to be services to invoke the Buddhas, so I joined the chant myself.[68] As I was leaving the Main Hall my gaze fell on the Hall of the Five Hundred Disciples [69] across the way. When I peered in, I saw that each of these holy figures (whatever sculptor had carved them) was different from all the others. People said that since there were so many you couldn't help discovering a familiar face among them. 'It may be true', I thought, looking carefully—at the very image, vivid to the life, of a man I had slept with when I was in my bloom!

As I stared, I realized that it was exactly like Yoshi-sama of Chōja-machi, a pleasure-quarter guest with whom I had exchanged vows of eternal love, and whose name was tattooed on a hidden part of my arm. But while I was thinking nostalgically of those days, I noticed a seated figure in a shadowy part of the alcove—a perfect copy of my master when I was a maidservant in uptown Kyoto. I could hardly forget the man after *that* episode!

Over on the other side I saw a man I used to live with, a certain Gobei, identical even to the same high nose. What made it all the more touching was that I'd been faithful to him for some time. Then I found myself gazing at the figure of a plump man dressed in pale blue, one shoulder bare. 'Who on earth could that gentleman be?' I wondered. . . . Of course!

XXIV. 'The Buddha's Five Hundred Disciples—All Very
     Familiar!'

    At the Great Cloud Temple. The man at the right kneels with prayer beads

(before a holy image), while a priest walks towards the Hall of the Five
Hundred Disciples. On the left the old woman looks in at the odd cluster of
saintly figures surrounding the statue of the Amida Buddha.

There was no mistaking Dambei of Kōji-machi, my secret lover on all my holidays while I served in Edo.

Further in, on the upper tier of the alcove, there was one whose saintly face had a fair complexion. I recognized him at once by his good looks: an actor from the river-bed theatre at Shijō. But although he'd been brought up as an entertainer, it was his luck to have *me* (during my long service at the tea-houses) for his very first woman! And I taught him all the tricks. Before long, he collapsed like a paper-lantern—and went out! At twenty-four he was carried off to the Toribeno grave-yard. His shrivelled chin and sunken eyes left no doubt about it. . . .

Another was a red-faced man with a moustache, and a bald head. Without the moustache I'd have taken him for that abbot who hounded me when I was a secret mistress at his temple. My body was used to any amount of foolishness; but after being tormented by him day and night, I began to suffer from a kind of consumption. Still, everyone has his limits. That virile gentleman himself went up in smoke.

Again, under a withered tree there was a clever-looking fellow who appeared to have given the tonsure to his own beetle-browed head. His arms and legs really seemed to move —he could all but speak. And with him, too, the more I looked, the more he reminded me of someone I'd once been fond of. Among the men I met while I was a singing nun (and met new ones every day) there was a certain warehouse official from the Western Provinces. He fell madly, recklessly in love with me— impossible to forget any of those griefs and joys! And he gave me what people part with most reluctantly, which put the old woman I worked for in an excellent humour.

Of all these five hundred figures, which I calmly inspected at my leisure, not a single one failed to remind me of a former lover. I looked back on the whole turbulent course of my past life.

Alas! I knew I had followed the most frightful of careers. 'How wretched and shameful of me to enjoy such a long life,' I thought, 'when I've spent it giving my body to more than ten thousand men!' At this, my heart began to pound like the rumbling of the fiery car [70] of Hell, and my tears were scattered like bubbles of boiling water. Instantly I went into a delirium.

Unaware even that I was in a temple, I fell writhing on the ground.

But then a number of priests gathered near me, and I heard, 'It's sunset already.' Startled by the ringing of the great temple bell, I finally came to myself again. 'Why are you in such grief, old woman?' they asked, very gently. 'Are you weeping because one of these saints looks like a departed child or husband?' That made me all the more ashamed.

Without a word I fled from the temple . . . and as I left its gate I experienced my great awakening. 'Though the name lingers, the form vanishes; bones turn to ashes lost in the grassy swamp.' [71] How true!

At last I came to the foot of Mount Narutaki. Since I had no one to leave behind on the path into the Mountains of Salvation, I yearned to cut myself loose from this earth, cross the Sea of Passions, and reach the shore of the other world. Resolved to throw myself into the pond there, I began running blindly towards it.

But I was intercepted by an old admirer. It was he who built this bamboo-thatched shelter for me. 'Let death choose its own time', he urged me. 'Purify your heart of all your past wickednesses, and follow the Way of the Buddha!'

I responded admirably, giving myself up wholly to prayer and meditation. This went on day in and day out—that is, till you gentlemen came to my humble dwelling and enticed me into scattering my wits with *sake*! And now I've been foolish enough to tell you this long story, though I know life itself is short.

Well, never mind! This confession has driven away the clouds that obscured the clear moon of my heart. Perhaps it has helped you to while away a spring night pleasantly. Since I am a woman who spent her life in love (and out of wedlock), there's no use for me to hide anything. And so I've told you the story of my life, from youth, when I blossomed like the lotus, to withered age.

You may call it a trick of my old trade—but how could my heart be so impure?

NOTES

Throughout this book ages are given by the Japanese count (adding about a year to the Western), and Japanese names in the Japanese order (the surname first), except in bibliographical reference to works in English.

PART ONE

The *Ukiyo-zōshi* and the Floating World

I. GENROKU

1. G. B. Sansom, *Japan: A Short Cultural History* (New York, rev. ed., 1943), p. 481.

2. Saitō Ryūzō, *Kinsei Nihon sesōshi* (Tokyo, 1925), pp. 96–97 and 105–6.

3. Evidence of good government (cf. p. 227, note 13). Cranes (here literally 'thousand-year-birds') are also of extremely good omen. For this passage, see the *Teihon Saikaku zenshū* (9 vols. to date, Tokyo, 1949–55; henceforth referred to as TSZ), vol. 3, p. 139.

4. *De facto* Shogun from 1568 to 1582.

5. *The History of Japan* (3 vols., Glasgow, 1906), vol. 3, p. 21.

6. Ibid., pp. 6–7.

7. Yosaburō Takekoshi, *The Economic Aspects of the History of the Civilization of Japan* (3 vols., London, 1930), vol. 2, pp. 251–5.

8. G. B. Sansom, *The Western World and Japan* (New York, 1950), p. 189.

9. Kaempfer, vol. 1, p. 263.

10. Takekoshi, vol. 2, p. 209.

11. *Ukiyo monogatari.*

12. *Tokugawa bungei ruijū* (12 vols., Tokyo, 1914–15), vol. 2, p. 335.

13. TSZ, vol. 1, p. 67. There was a dangerous stretch of rocky shore called Oya-shirazu ('Forgetting Parents'—the Japanese version of 'Every man for himself!') which travellers going along the coast of Suruga to Edo had to cross.

14. A Kyoto Pattern-book of 1714 (*Hinagata: Gion-bayashi*) gives 144 designs for ladies' kimono, each to be executed in luxurious style. 'Take, for example, the design entitled "Brocade of the Capital". On the lower half of the kimono is the bold outline of the tall gate of the Imperial palace with its lacquered doors, metal hinges, and elaborate tile roofs supported by carved pillars. A blossoming cherry tree hangs over the right corner, while on the left is a heavily loaded orange tree. On the shoulder of the kimono there is a representation of the covered driveway which the Imperial palanquin took to the Hall of the Purple Dragon. On the left sleeve is a design showing two attendants bringing in the palanquin.' (*Report of the Librarian of Congress, 1939: Division of Orientalia*, p. 282.)

15. Takekoshi, vol. 2, p. 244.

16. In *Wazoku dōjikun* (1710).

17. *Ekken jikkun* (2 vols., Tokyo, 1927), vol. 1, p. 504.

II. PLEASURES OF THE UKIYO

1. On the history of the puppet theatre, see Donald Keene, *The Battles of Coxinga* (London, 1951), pp. 12–31; on *kabuki*, Earle Ernst, *The Kabuki Theatre* (New York, 1956); and on official attempts to regulate the *kabuki*, Donald H. Shively, '*Bakufu* Versus *Kabuki*', *Harvard Journal of Asiatic Studies*, vol. 18 (1955), pp. 326–56.

2. See Donald H. Shively, *The Love Suicide at Amijima* (Cambridge, Mass., 1953), pp. 18–29.

3. 'The designations of rank differed from locality to locality, and from generation to generation, with the result that the Japanese language has accumulated a list of over four hundred and fifty terms for prostitute.' (Shively, *Love Suicide*, p. 21.)

4. Tsuji Zennosuke, *Nihon bunkashi* (7 vols., Tokyo, 1948–50), vol. 6, pp. 198–9.

5. See Kenji Toda, *The Ryerson Collection of Japanese and Chinese Illustrated Books* (Chicago, 1931), pp. 14–16.

6. Block-printing made possible the profuse illustration characteristic of Tokugawa popular books, as well as the closely related development of the *ukiyo-e* woodcut. See Chapter V.

7. Most of their authors were scholars, priests, noblemen, or samurai, writing in the medieval didactic tradition.

8. Written *c.* 1610–15. See p. 37.

9. *Usuyuki monogatari* (1st dated ed., 1632). The sad love tale of a young samurai and Princess Usuyuki, whose name means 'thin snow', symbolic of evanescence. When she dies, he attains religious enlightenment.

10. *c.* 1640. See p. 91.

III. SAIKAKU

1. *Kōshoku ichidai otoko.*

2. TSZ, vol. 7, p. 23.

3. *Nippon eitaigura.*

4. TSZ, vol. 7, pp. 172–3.

5. *Kōshoku ichidai onna.*

6. TSZ, vol. 8, p. 275.

7. TSZ, vol. 2, p. 151.

8. *Kindai Nihon bungaku taikei* (25 vols., Tokyo, 1928–34), vol. 1, pp. 12–56.

9. *Kōshoku gonin onna.*

10. 'What the Seasons Brought the Almanac Maker', tr. by Wm. Theodore de Bary in *Five Women Who Loved Love* (Tokyo, 1956), pp. 115–56. Intending to trap an impudent clerk, the almanac-maker's wife takes the place of one of her maids in bed. But she happens to fall asleep, and awakes too late to save her own honour. She therefore decides to go on with the affair. Finally, taking a suitcase full of money, she elopes with the young man.

11. From Section 13 of the famous miscellany *Tsurezure-gusa*, by Yoshida Kenkō (1283–1350).

12. De Bary, pp. 119–22.

13. 'Saikaku' is the best known of his several pen-names, but his real name is thought to have been Hirayama Tōgo. The most detailed and trustworthy source of information on Saikaku and his works is Noma Kōshin, *Saikaku nempu kōshō* (Tokyo, 1952); for further Japanese bibliography, see

Richard Lane, 'Postwar Japanese Studies of the Novelist Saikaku', *Harvard Journal of Asiatic Studies*, vol. 18 (1955), pp. 181–99.

14. Harry Levin, 'Literature as an Institution', *Accent* (1946), p. 165.

15. Arthur Waley, tr., *The Tale of Genji*, vol. 1 (London, 1925), p. 42.

16. TSZ, vol. 1, pp. 161–5.

17. TSZ, vol. 1, p. 228.

18. Nyogo-no-shima, familiar from its depiction in a number of erotic *ukiyo-e* albums.

19. Tales such as *The Two Nuns* (*Ninin bikuni*), a lugubrious *kana-zōshi* of which the earliest dated ed. is of 1663, or *The Three Priests* (*Sannin hōshi*), of the late fifteenth or early sixteenth century. In these the medieval sense of death, and of the need to 'forsake the world' in preparation for it, are poignantly expressed. However, Saikaku was not the first to relate the confessions of a courtesan: in the third part of the trilogy *Kindling Fire* (*Takitsuke*), *Charred Wood* (*Moekui*), and *Dead Ashes* (*Keshizumi*), published together in 1677, a former courtesan tells a young man the secrets of her past success.

20. *Wakoku hyakujo*. Reproduced in *Nihon fūzoku zue* (12 vols., Tokyo, 1914–15), vol. 1, and (on a smaller scale) in *Nihon meicho zenshū* (31 vols., Tokyo, 1926–29; henceforth NMZ), vol. 30, pp. 27–96. Cf. Toda, pp. 110–11.

21. *Wakoku shoshoku ezukushi*. In *Nihon fūzoku zue*, vol. 2, and NMZ, vol. 30, pp. 1–26. Cf. Toda, pp. 105–6.

22. *Honchō nijūfukō*.

23. *Erh-shih-ssu-hsiao* (read *Nijūshikō* in Japanese). Although it is not clear when this work was brought to Japan, a translation was published there early in the seventeenth century. The best of the *kana-zōshi* adaptations was Asai Ryōi's *Yamato nijūshikō* (1665).

24. TSZ, vol. 3, p. 135.

25. The famous scene of the fight between Benkei and Minamoto Yoshitsune, to whom he then swears allegiance. Such banners would be flown at the time of the Boys' Festival, the fifth day of the fifth month.

26. From a poem by Fujiwara Kanesuke in vol. 15 of the *Gosen wakashū*: *Hito no oya no/kokoro wa yami ni/aranedomo/ko o omou michi ni/madoinuru kana*. 'Parents with anxious hearts, even when there is no darkness, wander lost through the streets, thinking of their children.' *Yami* ('darkness', 'grief'), *michi* ('street', 'moral path'), and *madou* ('be lost', 'be perplexed') are used in both literal and figurative senses.

27. It may be helpful to list here the chief monetary units mentioned in these translations. Of course they often fluctuated in value; still, some notion of their purchasing power may be had from the numerous prices—of everything from chopsticks to courtesans—quoted in Saikaku and Kiseki.

The most valuable unit of currency in general circulation was the gold *ryō*, which was equal to 4 *bu* in gold, the *bu* in turn equal to 4 *shu*. Silver coins (also often diluted) were ordinarily weighed by the standard *momme* unit (3·75 grams); 1 *kan* (or *kamme*) was 1,000 *momme*; the *fun* was 1/10 of 1 *momme*. But the pierced copper cash, or *mon*, was the real currency medium of the people. In general, 1,000 *mon* (a sum which was also called 1 *kan*) equalled 15 *momme* of silver, and 1 gold *ryō* equalled 50 *momme* until 1700, 60 *momme* thereafter. This decreased value of silver coinage reflected the Genroku 'currency reform', a radical debasement of quality in order to meet the expenses of the Shogun Tsunayoshi. 'But the great expenditures and infusion of debased but plentiful coin at this time aided the further development of the Tokugawa coinage system as the economic standard for transactions not only in the cities and large towns but also throughout all the provinces.' (Norman Jacobs and Cornelius C. Vermeule III, *Japanese Coinage* [New York, 1953], p. 29.)

28. TSZ, vol. 3, pp. 139–40.

29. TSZ, vol. 3, pp. 167–8.

30. Kaempfer, vol. 3, p. 21.

31. See note 26 above.

IV. KISEKI AND THE HACHIMONJI-YA

1. Kiseki was his usual literary pseudonym, Ejima (or Ejimaya) a shop-name used as a surname; his actual surname is thought to have been Murase; at retirement he took the priestly name of Sōe. And he was ordinarily called Ichirōemon. For bibliographical information on Kiseki and his writings, see Howard S. Hibbett, 'Ejima Kiseki (1667–1736) and his *Katagi-mono*', *Harvard Journal of Asiatic Studies*, vol. 14 (1951), pp. 404–32.

2. NMZ, vol. 9, pp. 649–50.

3. The oldest extant Hachimonji-ya book is a *jōruri* text dated 1651.

4. *Yakusha kuchi-jamisen.*

5. *Yakusha-hyōbanki.*

6. Quoted in Mizutani Futō, *Shinsen Retsudentai shōsetsushi* (Tokyo, 1929), p. 326.

7. *Keisei iro-jamisen.*

8. Cf. Sansom, *Japan*, p. 493.

9. 'Powdered-tea' girl: one of the many terms for which interesting etymologies may be found. Cf. J. E. de Becker, *The Nightless City* (Yokohama, rev. ed., 1906), pp. 47–48: '*Sancha* was the old time word for powdered tea, nowadays known as *matcha* or *hikicha*. In ancient times ordinary leaf tea was infused by placing it in a bag, and shaking this bag about in boiling water until the liquor was extracted. In the Japanese the verb "to shake" is *furu*, but this word is also used (especially by courtesans) to mean— "to repel" or "manifest dislike to" a guest. Ground tea (*sancha*)—on the contrary—was not placed in a bag, but put right into the water, and therefore it required no shaking. The negative form of the word *furu* is *furazu*, and *furazu* has the sense not only of "not to shake" but "not to repel". In the *Dōbō-Goyen* it is stated that many of the better class courtesans were proud as peacocks, and in the zenith of their prosperity they would at times display marked antipathy to some of their guests, going so far as to repel (*furu*) the visitor altogether. The newly arrived courtesans who had been brought into the Yoshiwara from all parts of Yedo City were quite tractable and docile and did not attempt to rebuff (*furazu*) would-be guests and hence the name *Sancha-jorō* ("Ground-tea harlots").'

The terms *hikifune* and *shika* also designate courtesans of medium rank. The *hikifune* ('towboat') was so named because these girls attended the *tayū*, the 'great ships' of the pleasure harbours. *Shika* ('deer') is sometimes explained as a complicated pun: an old word for deer is *shishi*, which could be written with characters meaning 4–4, or '16', in allusion to the modest 16-*momme* fee of girls holding this rank.

10. NMZ, vol. 9, p. 197.

11. *Yūjo-hyōbanki.*

12. *Hyakunin jorō shina-sadame.* Reproduced in *Nihon fūzoku zue*, vol. 3, and NMZ, vol. 30, pp. 771–802. Cf. Toda, pp. 129–30.

13. *Keisei tamago-zake.*

14. *Fūryū kyoku-jamisen.*

15. *Keisei tsure-jamisen.*

16. *Keisei kintanki.* See p. 92.

17. Takano Tatsuyuki, in *Nihon bungaku zenshi* (13 vols., Tokyo, 1935–43), vol. 8, p. 622.

18. Quoted in *Kindai Nihon bungaku taikei,* vol. 5, Introduction, p. 9.

19. Fujii Otoo, in *Hyōshaku Edo bungaku sōsho* (11 vols., Tokyo, 1935–38), vol. 2, p. 110.

20. Fujii Otoo, *Edo bungaku kenkyū* (Kyoto, 1921), p. 338.

21. *Katagi-mono.*

22. *Seken musuko katagi.*

23. TSZ, vol. 3, p. 136.

24. See p. 48.

25. That is, since the founding of the Japanese Empire (traditionally 660 B.C.). NMZ, vol. 9, p. 693.

26. *Seken musume katagi.*

27. NMZ, vol. 9, p. 824.

28. *Ukiyo oyaji katagi.*

29. NMZ, vol. 9, p. 851.

30. NMZ, vol. 9, p. 867.

31. Benjamin Boyce, *The Theophrastan Character in England to 1642* (Cambridge, Mass., 1947), p. 105.

32. *Seken hahaoya katagi* (1752).

33. *Tōsei shosei katagi.*

34. *Seken tekake katagi.*

35. *Teikoku bunko* (50 vols., Tokyo, 1893–97), vol. 30, p. 173.

V. UKIYO-E AND GENROKU FICTION

1. '*Ukiyoye* prints were the direct outcome of the development of popular book illustrations, and not of the printed pictures that existed in Japan before the Keichō era (1596–1614). Most of the *ukiyoye* painters were print designers as well as book illustrators, and the relation between these two forms of printed pictures is inseparable.' (Toda, p. vii.)

2. Cf. Toda, pp. 93–112.

3. *Ueno no hanami no tei* (*c.* 1675).

4. *Yoshiwara no tei* (*c.* 1680).

5. Shibui Kiyoshi (*Shoki hanga* [Tokyo, 1954], p. 57) says that nearly all the large, horizontal prints attributed to Moronobu are now coming to be recognized as the work of Sugimura Jihei (*fl. c.* 1680–95).

6. Mizutani Yumihiko, *Kohan shōsetsu sōgashi* (Tokyo, 1935), pp. 44–84.

7. See Howard S. Hibbett, 'The Role of the Ukiyo-zōshi Illustrator', *Monumenta Nipponica,* vol. 13 (1957), pp. 67–82.

8. Mizutani, op. cit., p. 146.

9. *Nure-sugata aisome-gawa.*

10. James A. Michener, *The Floating World* (New York, 1954), p. 208. This survey of *ukiyo-e* history includes a discussion of *shunga*: Chapter xx, 'The Other Books'.

11. See Plate XI.

12. See Plate IX.

13. See Plate XXI. The *koto,* an aristocratic zither-like instrument of 13 strings, was favoured by ladies of genteel upbringing.

14. On this edition see Lane, 'Postwar Japanese Studies of the Novelist Saikaku', pp. 197–8.

15. *Kōshoku ichidai otoko*, II, 5.

16. 'Passers by' is linked to a phrase from a *Shinkokinshū* poem (cf. p. 228, note 38), and that, in turn, to a *samisen* song about a snow-like burst of cherry blossoms on Mount Yoshino.

17. TSZ, vol. 1, p. 69.

18. Cf. Noma Kōshin, *Saikaku shinkō* (Tokyo, 1948), p. 324.

19. Donald Keene, *The Japanese Discovery of Europe* (London, 1952), frontispiece (a reproduction of Saikaku's original illustration).

20. Waley, vol. 1, p. 85.

21. Reproduced in Helen C. Gunsaulus, *The Clarence Buckingham Collection of Japanese Prints: The Primitives* (Chicago, 1955), pp. 127–30.

VI. ECCENTRICITIES OF THE UKIYO-ZŌSHI

1. NMZ, vol. 9, p. 696.

2. Sarumaru-dayū, an early Heian poet with an unusually wrinkled face.

3. Here Kiseki has written the last part of the word *misojihitomoji* ('31 syllables', a poetic name for the classic *waka* verse-form) with a character which means onion—and thus suggests another *hitomoji*, this one a dialect word for a kind of onion. Hence, too, the association with 'deep-rooted' in the following sentence.

Any puns found in my translation will, I hope, indicate similar word-plays in the original text. Where translation fails, I have occasionally resorted to a footnote.

4. NMZ, vol. 9, p. 686.

5. For example, *chihayaburu* ('powerfully strong') is followed by *kami* in the sense of 'paper', instead of by the other *kami* ('divinity') for which it is the traditional epithet.

6. *Teikoku bunko*, vol. 27, p. 575.

7. TSZ, vol. 7, p. 46.

8. NMZ, vol. 9, p. 672.

9. *Lespedeza bicolor*, or 'bush-clover', one of the 'seven plants of autumn'.

10. NMZ, vol. 9, p. 676. The Ritsu ('Rules') Sect stressed monastic discipline.

11. To be sure, *haikai* was the freest of poetic styles: its critics demanded the use of '*haikai* words'—colloquial or Sino-Japanese words, customarily debarred from poetic diction. Thus the word *ukiyo-e*, a neologism which has its first prose occurrence in *The Man Who Spent His Life in Love* (1682), appeared in a *haikai* book published the year before. See Ebara Taizō, *Edo jidaigo no kenkyū* (Kyoto, 1947), p. 178.

12. NMZ, vol. 9, p. 763.

13. Often, though doubtfully, attributed to Karasumaru Mitsuhiro (1579–1638), nobleman, poet, calligrapher, and author of numerous *kana-zōshi*.

14. *Kankatsu Heike monogatari*.

15. *Kinsei bungei sōsho* (12 vols., Tokyo, 1910–12), vol. 7, p. 336.

16. *A History of Japanese Literature* (London, 1899), pp. 304–5.

17. 'Male-Who-Invites' and 'Female-Who-Invites', the legendary progenitors of the Japanese Empire.

18. Or Kūkai (774–835), the leading Buddhist priest of the Heian Period, a man credited with new achievements in nearly every branch of culture.

19. George Kitchin, *A Survey of Burlesque and Parody in English* (Edinburgh, 1931), pp. 2–3.

PART TWO

Figures of the Floating World

From *Characters of Worldly Young Women*, by Ejima Kiseki

1. NMZ, vol. 9, pp. 763–6. Most of the first paragraph has been taken by Kiseki from *The Woman Who Spent Her Life in Love* (TSZ, vol. 2, p. 297); a few lines in the third paragraph from the end echo lines translated on pp. 158 and 159.

2. A ninth-century Chinese girl who, after Buddhist enlightenment, supported her parents by walking through the town selling bamboo fish-baskets. She was a familiar subject for painting.

3. Heaped at either side of the carriage entrance of a great house on formal occasions, as a last touch of elegance.

4. Persons attending this Shinto ceremony wore elaborate costumes in the style of the Court nobility.

5. A popular style of coiffure for young ladies, affected also by Saikaku's heroine.

A Wayward Wife (*Seken musume katagi*, I, 2)

1. The T'ang emperor whose brilliant reign (712–56) ended in disaster.

2. For a Saikaku parallel to the opening passage, see TSZ, vol. 2, pp. 143–4.

3. Cf. TSZ, vol. 1, p. 407.

4. Cf. TSZ, vol. 1, p. 395. The passage that follows echoes one in Saikaku's *Kōshoku seisuiki*, IV, 1.

5. Famous volcanoes.

6. A kind of Hachijō silk, so named because one roll of it was worth as much as eight rolls of ordinary silk.

7. The hero of Chikamatsu's immensely successful play *The Battles of Coxinga*, which had opened the year before and was still running. To visit his castle would be to make a forbidden voyage to China.

8. *Taiko*, short for *taiko-mochi* (literally, 'drum-bearers'), male entertainers hired to flatter and amuse guests. Their lament on p. 110 gives some notion of their duties; they were also expert at performing comic or ribald songs and dances.

9. A supernaturally endowed hero who helped to establish the Han Dynasty in the third century B.C. One of his victories came when, by night, he quietly approached the enemy camp while playing a nostalgic melody on the reed-pipe. The next morning it was discovered that 6,000 of the 8,000 enemy soldiers had deserted.

10. Cf. TSZ, vol. 1, p. 252.

From *Characters of Worldly Young Men*, by Ejima Kiseki

1. NMZ, vol. 9, pp. 653 and 656–7.

2. The midsummer Buddhist Festival of the Dead.

3. See Chapter III, note 27. A very rough calculation suggests that this sum would equal the total annual net income of about 1,000 average peasants. (Cf. Shively, *Love Suicide*, pp. 106-7.)

4. About half of this paragraph is taken from Saikaku's *Everlasting Storehouse of Japan* (TSZ, vol. 7, p. 52); similarly, the latter half of the next paragraph and the beginning of the following one (TSZ, vol. 7, pp. 102-3).

A Spendthrift (*Seken musuko katagi*, I, 3)

1. Made of an unplaned strip of Japanese cypress. On the coins mentioned in the following paragraph, see Chapter III, note 27.

2. Made by Nagata Yūji, a Kyoto lacquer-worker of this period.

3. *Nagasu* ('to set adrift') also means 'to forfeit'.

4. Cf. TSZ, vol. 7, pp. 374-5.

5. *Kechimyaku*, a kind of written charm containing an abridged lineage of the transmitters of Buddhism. It was closely guarded during its possessor's life, and at his death put in the coffin with him.

6. *Hasami-bako*, a box fixed to one end of a pole, to be carried by a man-servant. It was ordinarily used to bring along changes of clothing on an outing.

7. As an offering, that is, or at a party, where courtesans only served their guests.

8. See p. 27.

9. An oblong gold coin with a face value of 1 *ryō*.

A Swaggerer (I, 2)

1. 'A demon in a priest's robe' (*oni ni koromo*) is the Japanese equivalent of 'a wolf in sheep's clothing'. On following passage cf. TSZ, vol. 3, p. 156.

2. Takeda Shingen (of Kai) and Uesugi Kenshin, his arch-rival, were among the most famous generals of the complicated wars of the sixteenth century. Shingen's lieutenant Yamamoto Kansuke was killed in one of their many indecisive engagements at Kawanakajima, in 1561.

3. A sage reputed to have taught the arts of strategy to Chang Liang (see p. 224, note 9).

4. There is here an allusion to the legendary exploits of Oguri Hangan (1398-1464), who tamed another such wild, man-eating horse. Yet—a realistic note—Kiseki's young man does not match Hangan's feat of making the horse climb a ladder.

A Prig (II, 1)

1. Cf. NMZ, vol. 2, p. 221.

2. The four primary texts of Sung Neo-Confucianism: *The Great Learning*, *The Analects*, *Mencius*, and *The Doctrine of the Mean*. Learning to read these texts aloud preceded any attempt to understand them.

3. A quotation (Legge tr., modified) from *The Analects* (I, 3).

4. *Analects*, XIII, 18.

5. Another name for the Sung Confucianist Ch'eng I (1033-1107).

6. Literally, 'writing-practice', used in association with 'scraps of waste paper'.

A Rake (V, 1)

1. About six days' journey from Osaka, in a different direction from Arima.

A Worthless Trio (II, 3)

1. Presented as gifts at spring and fall. Since they bore the crests of the lords who gave them, they made this man's richly hung clothes-racks look like illustrations in the *Mirror of Edo*, a work listing the crests, ranks, incomes, residences, vassals, etc., of all the *daimyō*.

2. *Edo kagami* (1659).

3. Kinds of highly prized tea-bowls.

4. *Morokoshi-bune*, an improper allusion to Morokoshi, a famous *tayū* of the Ichimonji-ya in Shimabara. It was not unusual to come by boat to certain of the gay quarters; here, though, besides the double meaning noted above, there is also an association with the later expression 'passed through many experiences', for which the Japanese idiom is, literally, 'to row offshore' (*oki o kogu*).

5. Near Ōtsu, about three miles east of Kyoto.

6. The licensed quarter of Ōtsu, which is on the south shore of Lake Biwa—hence the allusion to the 'lake of passion'.

7. Literally, 'one foot from eyebrow to eyebrow', the name of a man of unusual size and strength described in vol. 13 of *The Chronicles of the Great Peace (Taiheiki)*.

8. Cf. TSZ, vol. 3, p. 239.

9. The often-sworn-by Shinto gods of the mountains bearing these names.

10. 'Left to wait' (*sumō yori hoka ni tanoshimi nashi*) has the secondary meaning 'obsessed with the joys of wrestling', and serves as a pivot between these two sentences.

11. His were hand puppets, larger and more elaborate than the string-manipulated marionettes of the time.

12. See note 4 above. The 'promenade', (*dōchū*), in which a *tayū* and her entourage paraded within the licensed quarter, is illustrated in Plate III.

13. A relic of his wrestling career.

14. A metaphor of Buddhist causality, here alluding also to the actual wheels of the carts he had to pull.

From *The Woman Who Spent Her Life in Love*, by Ihara Saikaku

An Old Crone's Hermitage (*Kōshoku ichidai onna, I, 1*)

1. There is a French translation of I, 1–4 by Georges Bonmarchand in the *Jubiläumsband* of the Deutsche Gesellschaft für Natur- und Völkerkunde Ostasiens (2 vols., Tokyo, 1933), vol. 2, pp. 270–304; cf. also (for II, 1–4) J. Rahder in *Acta Orientalia*, vol. 13 (1934), pp. 292–318. A complete German translation by Satoshi Tsukakoshi with the collaboration of Max Niehans has appeared under the title *Kôshokumono* (Zurich, 1957).

2. A metaphor found in several Chinese sources, of which the earliest is the third century B.C. *Lü-shih ch'un-ch'iu* (I, 2).

3. 'Plum Ford', used in association with the 'flowers' of the next sentence.

4. See Chapter VI, note 9.

5. In the manner of a courtesan.

6. Reigned from 1429 to 1465.

7. A Shinto shrine convenient to the palace, and one in which all the deities were worshipped.

8. Over the Uji River, near the village of Uji, south of Kyoto. These lines allude to a poem by Fujiwara Sadayori (*Senzaishū*, vol. 6): *Asaborake/Uji no kawa-giri/taedae ni/arawarewataru/seze no ajirogi*. 'In the early morning mist on the Uji River, stretched across, dimly seen, the net-stakes in the shallows.'

9. Yamabuki no se, near the Uji Bridge. There are numerous word-plays in this paragraph.

Musical and Dancing Festivities (I, 2)

10. At the Tanabata Festival, beginning on the seventh day of the seventh moon. The name Komachi is here linked to an allusion to a poem by Ono no Komachi (*Kokinshū*, vol. 2): *Hana no iro wa/utsurinikeri na/itazura ni/waga mi yo ni furu/nagameseshi ma ni*. 'As flowers fade, I too, idle in the long rains, have grown old gazing on them.'

11. From 1658 to 1660.

12. Specifically, a *chōgin* silver coin weighing 43 *momme*.

Provincial Lord's Favourite (I, 3)

13. From the *nō* play *Takasago: kaze eda o narasanu* 'the wind does not sigh in the branches' (in the serene weather of a benevolent reign). But Saikaku has substituted Edo (the Shogun's capital) for *eda* ('branches').

14. *Yakumo tatsu*, a 'pillow-word' for Izumo, taken from a poem attributed to the god Susanoo and said to be the ancestor of all poetry in the classic 31-syllable *waka* form.

15. Probably an oblique reference to the Emperor Go-Daigo, who spent part of 1332 and 1333 in exile there.

16. A variant of the proverb '*koban* to a cat'—or 'pearls before swine'.

17. A Buddhist term for Paradise, used here in association with the earlier allusion to the Buddha, which was in turn suggested by the 'stone Buddha' of the proverb.

18. In Edo.

19. Flowers more beautiful than the most famous cherry blossoms of Japan, that is. This metaphor of exotic luxury suggests the sumptuous life of a Chinese emperor's favourite concubine.

20. A strong aphrodisiac, of which Yonosuke took fifty jars along on his voyage to the Island of Women.

Wanton Beauties (I, 4)

21. In 1641 it was transferred to the south-western Kyoto site of the present Shimabara.

22. The waning moon of the sixteenth night, mentioned in association with her age (somewhat late for apprenticeship as a courtesan) and with the poetic name 'Moon Capital' for Kyoto.

23. Supposedly a love-letter from a rival.

24. On which guests had to pay especially high rates and give large tips.

25. And who must therefore lead the other guests in every phase of the ritual.

26. The Chrysanthemum Festival, on the ninth day of the ninth month. One of the more important of the many 'special festival days'—see note 24 above.

27. Gathering it up in a loose tuft at the top of the head, the simplest kind of hair-dress.

28. *Hikifune* (cf. Chapter IV, note 9).

29. Girls of the third rank who were popular chiefly for their ability on the *samisen*.

30. *Mekari*, a *nō* play in which the role of *waki* ('the second actor') is unusually important. The Takayasu school of *nō* actors specialized in *waki* roles.

31. *Dainagon*, the title of a high though long-powerless Court official.

32. An early tenth-century poet, known chiefly as grandson of the famous Narihira and author of the first *waka* of the first Imperial anthology: the *Kokinshū*.

33. Autumn Wind—and 'was intimate with' (*ni shimite*) has in Japanese the further meaning 'was pierced by'.

34. Garments of this colour were forbidden by Bakufu regulation.

35. *Hagi* flowers (see Chapter VI, note 9) are often associated with lonely, amorous deer. 'The insignificant blossom of the straggling lespedeza shrub is a favourite, on account of ancient poetic fables touching the amours of the lespedeza, as a fair maiden, and of the stag her lover.' (Basil Hall Chamberlain, *Things Japanese* [London, 5th ed., rev., 1905], p. 174.)

Courtesan of Middle Rank (II, 1)

36. A large oblong gold coin with a face value of 10 *ryō*.

In the Lower Ranks of the Gay Quarter (II, 2)

37. Only samurai were allowed to carry the long sword with the short one. Here Saikaku is criticizing Bakufu attempts (in 1668 and 1683) to forbid townsmen even to carry short swords.

38. From a poem by Fujiwara Teika (*Shinkokinshū*, vol. 6): *Koma tomete/sode uchiharau/kage mo nashi/Sano no watari no/yuki no yūgure.* 'Nowhere to draw up my horse for shelter and shake the snow off my sleeves; a snowy evening at the Sano ferry.'

39. See p. 225, note 6.

40. *Tokoroten*, a favourite summer dish.

41. In Osaka.

42. The usual contract was for ten years, but it might be extended for a deeply indebted girl.

43. There was regular passenger-boat service on the Yodo River between Osaka and Fushimi (near Kyoto).

44. TSZ, vol. 2, p. 268.

Lady Etiquette-teacher and Letter-writer (II, 4)

45. Indications of an erotic temperament. Cf. p. 166.

46. An allusion to a popular song of the 'Silver Threads Among the Gold' variety. 'Growing old together, till you're 100 and I'm 99 . . .'

Maidservant of a Townsman (III, 1)

47. Traditionally eighteen days in normal years, but nineteen when an 'unlucky day' (as determined by the *yin-yang* theory) happened to fall within it. Such periods were expected to be particularly hot.

48. In the summer of 1685 some pretended exorcists of such a demon were exposed and punished.

49. Whale-oil was cheap, but unpleasant to the nose.

50. In Kyoto.

51. One of the 'Three Sights of Japan'. All the views she mentions are frequently cited in poetry.

52. Men who went into the mountains (in groups, during the summer months) to practise religious austerities.

53. In ordinary, uncoquettish fashion.

54. On the twenty-eighth day of the eleventh month religious ceremonies were observed in honour of the founder of the True Pure Land Sect.

55. The *kataginu*, or 'shoulder-piece', worn by believers of the True Pure Land Sect on holy occasions. Of course the *kataginu* was ordinarily worn over another formal garment: the *hakama* ('divided skirts').

56. An allusion to the dance at the end of the *nō* play *Sotoba Komachi*, in which the once-famous beauty Ono no Komachi—now old and hideous—is possessed by the ghost of one of her frustrated lovers. During the dance Komachi cries: 'Oh, how I love her!'

57. *Mai-ōgi*, a 'dance-fan', in further allusion to *nō* dancing. Her madness ends with a matter-of-fact parallel to the resolution of the *nō* play.

58. TSZ, vol. 2, p. 297.

59. A necessary step on the path to Buddhahood.

Ruined by Love in Ishigaki (V,1)

60. A cheap tea-house quarter in Kyoto, from which she sinks to one even worse. There is a play on the literal meaning of Ishigaki: 'stone wall'—crumbled by love.

61. As worn by very young girls.

62. The first and third lines of a poem familiar from the *Yuan-chi huo-fa*, a collection of source material for writing Chinese poetry.

63. Gansai Yashichi, Kagura Shōzaemon, Ranshu Yozaemon, and Ōmu Yoshibei were the so-called Four Heavenly Kings of the Kyoto jesters at that time.

64. TSZ, vol. 2, p. 343.

65. Ten *mon* for her favours, twelve for the umbrella.

66. Eight bells sounded at 2.00 A.M., 7 at 4.00 A.M.

67. TSZ, vol. 2, p. 368.

The Buddha's Five Hundred Disciples—All Very Familiar! (VI, 4)

68. A three-day annual ceremony, beginning on the nineteenth of the twelfth month. The names of all the Buddhas were intoned, and the sins of the year confessed and expiated.

69. The 500 *Rakan* (Arhat, 'one who has extirpated his passions'). 'These Worthies are continuously represented in Chinese and Japanese art, usually with haloes around their shaven heads, and enlarged ear-lobes, the sign of great wisdom, singly or in groups, sometimes treated in a scandalously satirical manner, but owing to a want of uniformity as to the emblem borne by each, identification is often attended with great difficulty.' (Will H. E. Edmunds, *Pointers and Clues to the Subjects of Chinese and Japanese Art* [London, 1949], p. 226.) Among them are often seen a seated figure holding a begging bowl in both hands, another studying a scroll, and another leaning forward against a staff.

70. A kind of burning chariot in which sinners are transported in one of the Buddhist Hells.

71. From a poem by Su Tung-p'o.

INDEX